CORNELL STUDIES IN ANTHROPOLOGY

FRUITLAND, NEW MEXICO:

A Navaho Community in Transition

Cornell Studies in Anthropology

This series of publications is an outgrowth of the program of instruction, training, and research in theoretical and applied anthropology originally established at Cornell University in 1948 with the aid of the Carnegie Corporation of New York. The program seeks particularly to provide in its publications descriptive accounts and interpretations of cultural process and dynamics, including those involved in projects of planned cultural change, among diverse aboriginal and peasant cultures of the world.

Fruitland, New Mexico:

A Navaho Community in Transition

BY

TOM T. SASAKI

The University of New Mexico

Cornell University Press

ITHACA, NEW YORK

92491

This work has been brought to
publication with the assistance of
a grant from the Ford Foundation.

First published 1960

PRINTED IN THE UNITED STATES OF AMERICA

BY THE VAIL-BALLOU PRESS, INC.

To MYRT

Preface

THIS book is based on field data collected by the author and research workers who were attached to the Cornell University Southwest Project. The author was associated with the Project from 1948 to 1956. Since his and his co-workers' relationships with the Indians and the Indian Service affected and were affected by the changing cultural milieu, a résumé of field contacts and methods is given here.

Before entering the Fruitland community in 1948, the writer obtained permission from the superintendent of the Navajo Reservation. Because of a very tense situation then existing, the superintendent suggested that the writer live in government quarters and phoned the local supervisor to arrange for housing. Unfortunately, the superintendent did not explain the purpose of the proposed research, and in view of the tensions between the Navahos and the local agency, the writer decided to dissociate himself from the supervisor so as not to be identified with him.

The Navahos, even after hearing that the proposed research concerned their farming methods, believed the writer to be an investigator of their complaints against the Agency and especially its campaign against surplus horses. When asked about their farming methods, they spoke instead of their problems with the government.

Authenticated reports indicated that there were rumors that the writer was an enemy spy, intent upon learning the Navaho language. The Fruitlanders remembered that during the war against the Japanese many Navahos in the Marine Corps were employed in field communications, using their own language. Young Fruitlanders, especially those who had served in the armed forces, now mistrusted the author's loyalty, and he found himself consciously avoiding any study of the language. They, in turn, judiciously avoided the writer. The time came when he had to make the first of a series of defenses of his loyalty, but before then news spread among the Fruitlanders that certain agency personnel were against the author. This they took as meaning that the writer was "for" them, although his position was in actuality neutral.

The author's principal objective through the summer of 1948 was to establish sufficient rapport so that he could return the following year. He hired an interpreter recently discharged from the Marine Corps and a second veteran who agreed to serve on a stand-by basis. Both were well known in the farming area closest to the administration headquarters. This facilitated entree into Unit 2, considered by government employees as the most antagonistic. Having no transportation, the author and his interpreters walked from one farmhouse to the next; by the end of six weeks almost all farmers with land assignments in that unit were interviewed.

Contacts with residents of Unit 1 were the result of a series of fortunate circumstances. As part of an investigation of the horse-reduction program the chief animal husbandman from Window Rock visited Fruitland. The supervisor, the Tribal Council delegate, the animal husbandman, and the author visited some fifty farm families in Unit 1 to solicit their views on the number of horses required to farm ten acres. Throughout this survey, the writer, after being introduced as "from an Eastern university," served as recorder and, when the interviews were completed, was allowed to ask questions. Thus he obtained information not only about the number of horses each farmer needed for farming, but about off-reservation work experiences, household composition, farming implements, and so on. During the last week of the summer, Dr. G. William Skinner, then a graduate student, joined the author with a car, and further interviewing in Unit 1 became possible. Information concerning crop production, assignees' names, and the like was obtained from the supervisor.

In April of the following year the writer returned to the Southwest Project. There had been changes in personnel. And there was considerably less tension in the community. People who had been contacted the previous summer were cordial, and those who spoke English seemed less constrained. In July and August, Elizabeth Green and John Musgrave joined in the research, as did other students and trainees through the following six years.

Fieldworkers gathered data principally through the use of open-ended interviews. But, in addition, they also made extensive notes on the meetings that they attended. Observations of behavior were also recorded at "squaw dances" and other ceremonials, in work groups, at trading posts and stores, and at rodeos and fairs both off and on the reservation. Notes were also made on the daily and weekly round of life of selected families with whom rapport had been more firmly established. Lest the sample be unrepresentative, new fieldworkers were instructed to enlarge upon it. Since the author's contacts were now fairly extensive, he facilitated the entree of new personnel by introducing them to Fruitlanders in key positions. Having thus established their initial contact, fieldworkers sought their own informants. Almost all adult men and a smaller proportion of women were interviewed at least once.[1]

Data were also obtained through the survey method, varying from highly unstructured to more rigidly structured designs. In addition to the horse-ownership survey, loosely structured surveys were conducted on English-speaking skills and on housing. The most rigid in design was that employed by Dr. Gordon F. Streib in 1950 and 1951, in a study of the serviceability of the survey method itself among Navahos, with comparative data from Many Farms, another small irrigated farming community in the interior of the reservation.[2]

Fieldworkers also collected life histories. Intensive interviews were held with informants who consented to tell the researchers about their early life. But since most able-bodied Navahos were busy, it was not possible to get lengthy statements. There was less difficulty in obtaining current data. Considerable historical and current information about thirty Fruitlanders was collected, assembled, and filed.

Several other sources of information were tapped: government records, local newspapers including old files, and minutes

[1] Notes were typed on hectograph duplicating stencils after each interviewing or observational session. These were then coded and mailed to Cornell University, where they were reproduced; sections were trimmed to fit 5 x 8 cards, attached to these cards, and filed under the coded categories. Full notes by fieldworkers were also bound together in chronological order under the name of each interviewer so that the full context of the items on the coded 5 x 8 cards would be readily available. See Appendix A for the category system used.

[2] Tom T. Sasaki and David L. Olmsted, "Navaho Acculturation and English-Language Skills," *American Anthropologist*, n.s. LV (1953), 89–99; Marc-Adelard Tremblay, John W. Collier, Jr., and Tom T. Sasaki, "Navaho Housing in Transition," *Americana Indigena*, XIV (1954), 187–219; Gordon F. Streib, "The Use of Survey Methods among the Navaho," *American Anthropologist*, n.s. LIV (1952), 30–40.

of Fruitland community meetings. Interviews were held with government officials and with traders and others on the north side of the river and in town.

Thus the field methods were devised to secure information on several dimensions: intensive studies of individual personalities and of families and the intercultural contact situation—all in historical and current perspective.

Although there was no formal agreement between Cornell University, the Bureau of Indian Affairs, and the Navaho tribe until 1952 (see Appendix B for the proposed working agreement, which was eventually established), members of the research team were called occasionally by the Indian Field Service for consultation on an informal basis, which led to good relations with administrators. Eventually agency personnel at Fruitland and at Shiprock came to look upon Cornell researchers with less suspicion; local community leaders and those on the tribal level also became friendly. In this way the researchers could exchange ideas, discuss plans, play the role of sounding board, and occasionally suggest a new approach. Because of a certain rigid quality in the structure and functioning of the Bureau, a frontal attack (with published articles and "reports on conditions") seemed likely to be disastrous to rapport and hence to effectiveness. Differences in orientation between Indian Bureau technicians, whose aim it was to get things done, and the researchers' interest in testing hypotheses which emerged from the empirical situation prevented convergence into projects that could be set up as experiments. Furthermore, the researchers were not continuously in the field. Therefore, although field officials used some of the ideas suggested, the author was not always in a position to test their efficacy rigorously.

The researchers' role in the community was never clear to the Fruitlanders. They had had no experience with anthropologists, who seemed to spend their time in no productive activity.[3] The explanation that Cornell offered courses on the American Indians, that its students were interested in the Navahos' situation, and that the primary purpose was to learn "first hand how they were making out on their farms" and how the Navaho way of life in the old days compared to that today was not enough. It was also necessary to tell Fruitlanders what the researchers did not represent—that they were not affiliated with the Indian Bureau and were not in a position to help them directly through influence on policy or through obtaining material aid for them.

The writer and his fellow researchers were, however, able to offer personal services and to participate in Navaho life as much as possible. They drove expectant mothers and others to the hospital; transported whole families to fairs, rodeos, fiestas, and the Gallup ceremonials; wrote letters and aided in filling out mail-order blanks; helped to bale alfalfa, plow and irrigate fields, clean ditches, and herd sheep; typed petitions and listened to issues community leaders wished to air; took medicine men to seek herbs. In return the Navahos answered questions, offered meals and sometimes cash (for expenses and gas) after trips, and invited the researchers to such social events as horse races and weddings.

Although the personal services sometimes impeded formal interviewing, they nevertheless provided opportunities to observe and to formulate lines of inquiry which would not otherwise have emerged. Moreover, such relationships were almost mandatory since informants were not paid—a necessary policy both because of the then high wage rate (a dollar an hour) and because it was hoped that the Fruitlanders, expecting benefits

---

[3] Since words such as "research," "experiments," and "survey" had unfavorable connotations, they were avoided. Although the Navahos never directly used these words and although government officials too perhaps never used them, they unavoidably became associated with "reduction" (of stock). See E. H. Spicer, ed., *Human Problems in Technological Change* (New York: Russell Sage Foundation, 1952), pp. 185–207.

other than cash, might be more likely to participate in action programs planned as part of the research.

Deep appreciation should be expressed to all members of the field staff for their conscientious work and for use of their field data. The Southwest Project is part of the Cornell Studies in Culture and Applied Science, a program of research and training; acknowledgment is here made for the support given the program by the Carnegie Corporation of New York. The total program is directed by Lauriston Sharp. The Southwest Project is under the general supervision of Alexander H. Leighton. John Adair served as field director between 1949 and 1952, the author between 1952 and 1956.

I wish to express my appreciation to the following for their valued criticisms and suggestions on the various sections of the manuscript: John Adair, Allan R. Holmberg, Clyde Kluckhohn, Morris E. Opler, Lauriston Sharp, and Robin M. Williams, Jr.

To Alexander H. Leighton, who was responsible for the initiation of the Southwest Project and whose inspiration and guidance throughout have been invaluable, I am especially indebted. I also express my appreciation to Professor Leighton, to Robert J. Smith, and to W. W. Hill for their critical suggestions on the total manuscript and for seeing it to its publication.

Acknowledgment is made of professional help received in reorganizing and rewriting the manuscript and also of editorial assistance by Robert Bunker and Dale Evans. Thanks are due Tazu Warner and Myrtle Sasaki for typing the manuscript.

For the co-operation and the time extended to me and to members of the Cornell Southwest Project by numerous Bureau of Indian Affairs officials—John Collier and Dillon Myers, former Commissioners of Indian Affairs; Glenn L. Emmons, Commissioner of Indian Affairs; and most particularly to Wade Head, Mel Helander, Jerry Kessee, and Walter Olson of the

Gallup Area Office; the late Allan Harper, Warren J. Spaulding, Robert Young, and Howard Johnson of the Window Rock Navajo Agency; Elvin Jonus, Deb Victor, Vernon Hines, George McColm, Hobart Johnson, Kenneth Hamilton, Steven Henderson, Charles Schaeffer, and the late Babe Eaves—I wish to express my indebtedness.

To the late Jack Cline, Polly Cline, and Ken and Jan Brown, for the courtesy and hospitality given me and my family, and to other members of the research staff, I am grateful.

For the photographs used in this book, I give thanks to John W. Collier, Jr.

Deep appreciation is also expressed to the Navaho Indians of Fruitland who took me in as their friend and without whose co-operation the field work could not have been carried out. To Paul Jones, current chairman of the Tribal Council; Sam Ahkeah, former chairman; J. Maurice McCabe, secretary to the Navaho tribe; and the Fruitland councilmen, Hosteen Yellowman and Walter Collins—to all of these for their co-operation and help I express my gratitude.

The courtesy of the following publishers in granting permission to reprint materials from their copyrighted works is also acknowledged: American Philosophical Society, Bureau of Business Research of the University of New Mexico, The University of Chicago Press, Harper & Brothers, Harvard University Press, The Peabody Museum, Princeton University Press, *Social Research*, the Society for Applied Anthropology, and Yale University Press.

Tom T. Sasaki

Albuquerque, New Mexico
January 1960

Contents

Illustrations

Map

FRUITLAND, NEW MEXICO:

A Navaho Community in Transition

CHAPTER I

An Introductory
Perspective

THE Fruitland Irrigation Project extends for a distance of some twenty miles along the south side of the San Juan River in northwestern New Mexico.[1] The Project begins at the head gate about three miles west of Farmington and continues westward until the last farm is reached just west of the Hogback, a sharp sandstone ridge about five miles east of the settlement of Shiprock. The width of the Project varies from a few hundred yards

---

[1] For purposes of local administration the 15,000,000-acre Navajo Reservation (in northwestern New Mexico, northeastern Arizona, and southern Utah) and nearby areas, lands held in trust by the United States for the exclusive use of the Indians, are divided into nineteen districts. The Indian Bureau administrative unit which includes the Fruitland Project is Land Management District 13, consisting of 396,000 acres which are bounded on the north by the San Juan River, on the east by the nonreservation land of District 19, and on the west and the south by Districts 12, 14, and 15. In 1954 five subagencies were created, each administered by a subagency superintendent. Fruitland then became part of the Shiprock Subagency for administrative purposes. (The official federal government spelling is Navajo. This book follows the more common spelling, Navaho, for other than governmental designations.)

to about a mile, depending largely upon the winding of the sharply rising bluff to the south of the river. At three points the river meets the bluff, dividing the Project into three distinct units. The three communities are, however, linked by graded roads, and they draw water from a single large canal.

Running the length of the Fruitland Project on the north side of the San Juan River are irrigated farms belonging to non-Navahos.[2] These originate at the Hogback and run eastward through three unincorporated villages, Waterflow, Fruitland, and Kirtland,[3] and thence through the towns of Farmington and Aztec.

Until 1951 a footbridge located at Fruitland and a vehicular bridge on the eastern end of the Project near Farmington were the Navahos' only all-weather links with the highway, the villages, and the towns. (In that year the El Paso Natural Gas Company replaced the footbridge with an automotive bridge of steel and concrete.) During low water it was always possible to cross the river on horseback or by wagon. The Fruitland Navahos went across the river to patronize small stores [4] and sometimes churches, to work for non-Navaho farmers (and sometimes thus to learn about new plants and new techniques), or to join in the rodeos, the wrestling and boxing matches, and

[2] The non-Navaho farmers have larger holdings (averaging about 30.4 acres per farm in 1950, according to the 1950 *United States Census of Agriculture*, vol. I [part 30], p. 44) than those found on the south side; their technology is more advanced; their yields are higher. They have customarily hired up to thirty or more Navaho men, women, and children at harvest time.

[3] Kirtland is across the river from Unit 1, Fruitland across from Unit 2, and Waterflow slightly to the east of Unit 3.

[4] Of the eight trading posts across the river, three appeared to be visited more frequently than the others during the period of this study. One of these is near Unit 3 (accessible only when the river was low); the other two are almost directly north of Unit 2. Several trading posts in Farmington served customers who lived in Unit 1. Of the trading posts on the reservation which served the community, one is located in Unit 2, the others farther south at Carson and at Burnhams.

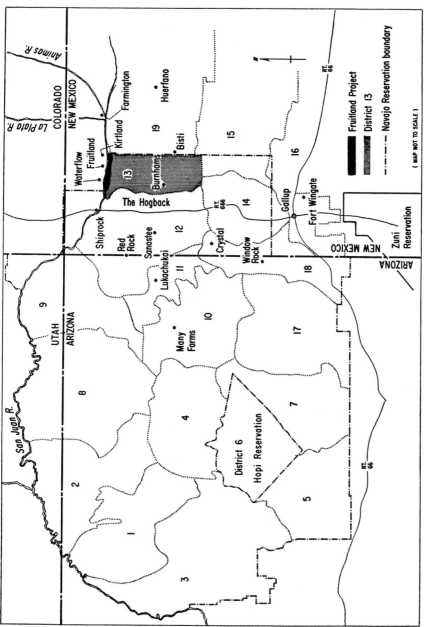

Map 1. Navajo Country

Legend:
- Fruitland Project
- District 13
- Navajo Reservation boundary

(MAP NOT TO SCALE)

the barbecue of the Pioneers' Day celebrations of the Mormons. Some of their non-Navaho neighbors attended the "squaw dances"[5] or horse races on the Navaho side of the river, and a few came as missionaries.[6]

Except along the riverbed, the region is 80 to 90 per cent desert or semidesert.[7] The elevation is 5,100 feet above sea level at Fruitland and over 6,000 feet on the rise above the river.[8] In the average year there are about 210 clear days, 80 partly cloudy days, and 70 cloudy days. Evaporation over the region proceeds rapidly under the influence of cloudless skies, low relative humidity, and gentle to moderate winds.[9] The average annual rainfall is 6.65 inches. Most of the precipitation takes the form of summer downpours of high intensity and short duration. The mean annual temperature according to the Fruitland weather station is 57.7 degrees Fahrenheit. Its maximum average is 68.8 degrees, and its minimum average 34.8 degrees. Extreme temperatures vary between 110 degrees above and 21 degrees below zero.[10]

The average growing season at Fruitland is limited to 156 days, with the last killing spring frost around May 6 and the first killing fall frost around October 9; freezes in late spring and early fall have sometimes cut the growing season to 114 days.[11] In so unpredictable a climate fruitgrowers expect to

[5] In this social aspect of the Enemy Way ceremonials maidens dance. See also p. 48.

[6] More often, however, missionaries have come from Arizona and Utah. The Mormons believe the American Indians to be one of the lost tribes of Israel. The Indians are considered to be "Lamanites," who sinned on arrival in the New World and whose skins became darkened. In order to enter heaven, the Indians must be converted to Mormonism, so these missionaries believe.

[7] "General Statement of Conditions in the Navajo Area" (mimeographed; Window Rock, Ariz.: Navajo Service, 1941), p. 31.

[8] *The Navajo Yearbook of Planning in Action*, Report no. V (Window Rock, Ariz.: Navajo Service, July, 1955), p. 56.

[9] "General Statement of Conditions in the Navajo Area," p. 29.

[10] *Ibid.*, pp. 16–17.   [11] *Ibid.*, p. 28.

harvest an apple crop only every other year and a peach crop only every third year.

Irrigation water from the San Juan enters the main canal (constructed in the mid-1930's) at the head gate and flows westward through the Project until the canal again joins the San Juan four miles beyond the Hogback, some eighteen miles down river. Individual farms receive water from the main canal through laterals constructed by the government around 1940, each lateral delivering water to a dozen or more farms. The canal can draw enough water to supply all the farms on the Project, if the farmers use the water wisely. Seasonal rainfalls and spring runoffs in the mountains of Colorado, draining into the Animas, the La Plata, and the San Juan rivers, ordinarily provide sufficient water. In the occasional dry seasons, many farms suffer from lack of moisture. During exceptionally wet years or when early warm weather melts the mountain snowpack rapidly, the head gate may become so heavily silted by freshets that delivery of water to the farm is delayed. Erosion is active on the farms, and silt is poured into the San Juan. Periodic sluicing is necessary to keep the canal flowing, and this is done every other week.[12]

In 1950 the Project included some 2,500 acres of irrigated land divided into 205 farms,[13] assigned by the Bureau of Indian Affairs to the male heads of 191 family units. (The productive acreage was less than the total number of acres because Fruitlanders set aside a half to one acre of land for homesites and corrals.) Each farmer fenced his assignment with four strands of barbed wire in accordance with Project regulations.

Although approximately 200 families, including some without farms, had homes at Fruitland, the Project population was not

[12] The irrigation water is drained back into the San Juan through sluice gates set at various points along the canal. Through this operation the silt drawn into the canal at the head gate is poured back into the river.

[13] Taken from a report, "Crop Production Record," compiled by a U.S. Indian Service agent at Fruitland, 1948.

stable, except in the summer. In 1950 the actual number of families who lived at Fruitland varied between thirty and forty during the winter months, when most were engaged in wagework off-reservation or on the plateau to the south at their winter homes. Fruitlanders also made numerous minor excursions away from the Project during the growing season. Throughout the spring and summer months railroad companies sought men for track maintenance work, and large farm corporations recruited labor for the carrot harvest. Some Navaho farmers left for temporary wagework when they had completed most of their heavy farm work or when they felt that their harvests were unlikely to meet expectations. The number who left at any one time was small, largely because late spring and summer was the season of the squaw dance; Navahos like to see their friends on these occasions and, by participating in the curing rites, hope to counteract the effects of alien forces encountered off-reservation during the winter. In years of normal rainfall the Project was practically deserted during September and October, when the harvesting of corn and final cuttings of alfalfa were the only remaining work. During this time 60 to 70 per cent of Fruitland adults found temporary employment in the pinto-bean fields in the vicinity of Cortez and Dove Creek, Colorado.

Population statistics for Navahos were formerly poor, but the assignment system at Fruitland has resulted in more reliable information.[14] Of 1,182 residents in Fruitland, specific data on the ages of 809 persons were available through the census or

[14] Records are fairly accurate if one considers that written materials were lacking until recent years. Dates of birth among older people are usually linked with some event which can be traced, but there are a few people eligible for old-age compensation who have not received it because the records show them as much as ten years younger than their real age. Unless one is familiar with the members of the particular family or with kinship terms, it is difficult to determine from the records even the sex of the person to whom a particular birth date or age is attributed.

school record. The age distribution of Fruitlanders in 1955 is shown in Chart 1. Almost 63 per cent were less than 20 years of age, and more than half were between 10 and 19. The population is thus seen to be weighted heavily on the side of younger

Chart 1. Age distribution by sex, 1955
(N = 809)

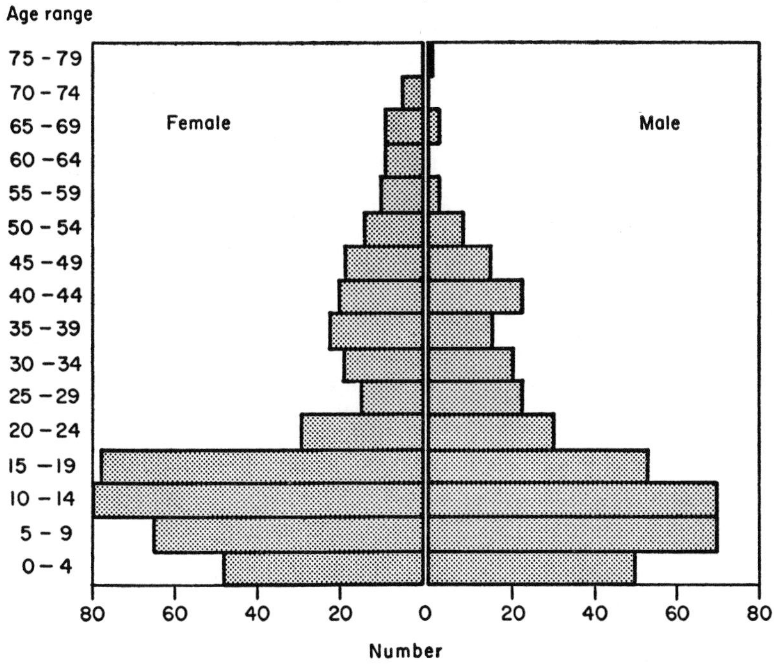

Age range

people, who have many years of productive life ahead of them.

The system of limited self-government at Fruitland is presided over by elected officials, including two delegates to the Tribal Council (concerned chiefly with the affairs of the whole tribe) and three officers, one from each of the Project's farming units chosen for a chapter organization (which deals primarily with local problems).[15] Tribal policemen carry out law enforcement duties from regional headquarters at Shiprock.

[15] The present form of tribal government has been in existence since 1938. The first efforts to develop an organization that would enable the

The Bureau of Indian Affairs is responsible for the administration of the technical aspects of the Irrigation Project. Besides the irrigation engineer, the Bureau provides agricultural technicians and schoolteachers. Stationed at Fruitland as permanent employees are the supervisor of the District, the irrigation engineer, the farm-management supervisor, the principal of the school, and his staff of teachers.

The fact that the Project was located close to the town of Farmington must be considered at this point. Although relationships between the Navahos and the people of Farmington were primarily economic, the town also served the Navahos very much as small towns anywhere serve rural folk. On Saturdays they shopped and gossiped there. Like other minority groups in the Southwest, they spent most of their time at places congenial to them but apart from the main flow of social life in the community. In particular, they patronized the traders and the bootleggers in the outskirts of the business section on one of the main roads leading to the Project.

In 1950 the Fruitland Project is seen as a relatively quiet and moderately prosperous little enclave of agrarian Indian life within the larger American culture. A gradual process of acculturation and assimilation had been under way for many years, undoubtedly accelerated by the effects of World War II; but many of the old attitudes still lingered on, in sharp contrast with new

---

tribe to deal with its growing problems date back to the treaty period beginning in 1868, followed by further attempts in 1923 when the discovery of oil at Shiprock made it imperative that a body be created which could speak for the tribe as a whole. In 1925 small units called "chapters" were instructed to elect officers and to handle their local business through them. The men elected to the offices were usually those who held views not acceptable to the majority of the Navahos, and as a result the chapter system collapsed in most communities. Where the chapters have continued, as at Fruitland, they have become centers of antigovernment gossip and agitation. (See Clyde Kluckhohn and Dorothea C. Leighton, *The Navaho* [Cambridge: Harvard University Press, 1946], pp. 100–105.)

habits adapted from the outside. During the spring and early summer, farmers for several years returned from off-reservation wagework. As the summer wore on, the English words of popular songs from the white culture, such as "Hubba Hubba Hubba," "Working on the Railroad," and "Living with a Widow in Winslow," could be heard at squaw dances. Concern was expressed by the older people over the generally un-Navaho behavior of participants and singers at ceremonials. Extra-marital sexual activities and excessive drinking at squaw dances were particular causes of alarm.

It was still difficult to cross to the north side of the river or to reach town. The swinging footbridge continued to serve Units 2 and 3. Since there were only twelve vehicles, most Navahos traveled the dirt road into town on Saturdays via buses, wagons, or horseback. Their contacts with non-Navahos were still mainly with traders. Occasionally they conducted business with the town blacksmith or visited the hospital or a doctor. When in town, the older Fruitlanders sunned themselves near the railroad tracks south of the trading posts; the young hung around the two pool halls (if they spoke no English) or went to ball games or to motion-picture shows. After dark, old and young men found bootleggers and either drank their liquor (usually muscatel wine) in the alleys or took the bottle home to share among friends. On Monday the police phoned the Fruitland trader that Mack Begay wanted bail or that the tribal policemen were in search of a husband who had beaten up his wife. In other words, general peace and tranquillity prevailed in Fruitland.

Within this quiet little community a tremendous social explosion, which would shake the structure of Navaho society to its foundations, was about to take place. The primary cause of this explosion was the construction of a natural-gas pipeline across 240 miles of reservation land. In the course of this construction, more than eighty Fruitland farmers were hired as unskilled laborers. Almost immediately there followed a vast influx of prospectors, drillers, and construction workers, which increased the population of nearby Farmington from 3,500 in 1950 to over 12,000 in 1952. For two years nearly every able-bodied Fruitlander had full-time employment, and farming was neglected. Navahos began to buy most of their food and clothing in town stores and to purchase such other items as wrist watches and automobiles. With new cars and money for gasoline, they not only moved about inside the reservation, but visited town more frequently than before. Lessons learned away from home were put into immediate practice, with varying effects.

There was a strong tendency for the Navahos already most accustomed to the new ways to increase the differences between themselves and their neighbors. The comparative newcomers in Fruitland, who had arrived only at the start of the Irrigation Project, integrated their behavior to non-Navaho norms more rapidly than did the members of long-established local kinship groupings. Young people, especially those who had attended off-reservation boarding schools, accepted new patterns of behavior far more quickly than their elders—and speeded developments by sending more children off to school. Of the 25,000 children in school by 1955 (four times as many as in 1950), one-half were in boarding schools far from the reservation.[16]

Each year the gap between older and younger Navahos has widened. With the death of more of the older men, the young have had fewer and fewer models at home on whom to pattern their behavior. But although they have shifted largely to a non-Navaho frame of reference, they see only confusedly what non-Navaho values and norms may be.

The character and implications of this explosive change in the mores of Fruitland are to be the main topic of this book. But first an examination is advisable of the background of the

[16] *The Navajo Yearbook of Planning in Action*, Report no. V, 1955, pp. 4–18.

community which in itself was the product of at least three major upheavals that had taken place within the last quarter century.

The first two upheavals were closely interconnected. During the early 1930's, nationwide crop surpluses and widespread droughts and dust storms throughout the Western states induced the federal government to embark on a vast program of stock reduction. By forced sales, the Navaho residents of Fruitland were compelled to reduce their ownership of sheep, cattle, and horses by as much as 50 per cent. So far as the overgrazed and eroded grasslands of the area were concerned, this reduction constituted a relief. For the Navahos, whose economy had been centered for many generations on grazing animals and who had always placed great emphasis on the possession of sheep and horses as a symbol of social success, the government's policy threatened immediate disaster. Their supreme and securest form of wealth had been cut off. By way of softening the blow, the government began a program to develop irrigation projects, in the course of which the irrigation canal at Fruitland, with its lateral canals, was finally completed in the period 1938–1940. Several unforeseen difficulties complicated the transition from a grazing to an agricultural economy. In an effort to spread the benefits of the new irrigation system as widely as possible, the government settled a hundred new Navaho families in the Fruitland area. The hundred long-time resident families bitterly resented this intrusion and expressed their antipathy against the new settlers directly and against the government. When the Agency announced that land allotments would be limited to ten acres per family, both newcomers and old-time residents were convinced that the whole scheme was an agency plot to depress the economic level of the people and to keep the Navahos in a perpetual state of poverty. Resentment was particularly apparent among the old-time residents. Many Fruitlanders had the impression that the government had "promised" each family a plot of twenty acres. When newcomers were located in the Project, these twenty-acre plots were reduced to ten acres or less, with all unused land to be assigned to newcomers and hence no longer available for replacing lands damaged by alkali seepage or for young Fruitlanders when they came of age. Widespread doubt existed that a Navaho family could feel secure of the tenure even of its ten-acre plot; the government might any day find reasons for taking this away. Thus one man stated that the government "wants to take everything away from the Navahos. He wants to keep cutting them down, down, and down." Deprived of their cattle and horses, pushed toward an occupation that they had not chosen, and provided with wholly inadequate means of support, The People, as they call themselves, felt that their only future was slow starvation.

Thus the two policies—the reduction of livestock in exchange for land and the dispersal of land assignments over a greater number of families—caused great concern among the original farmers. Within the community there was an increase in witchcraft gossip and other forms of social control which served to relegate the newcomers to a subordinate position. Against the government, attitudes of opposition and hostility were expressed only verbally. For the most part The People merely avoided contact with the government agents because of the Navahos' belief that the "government was against them." As one man said, "I always stayed away because there was no use trying to talk." To add to the confusion, non-Navahos nearby voiced their opinions regarding government policy, and some, under the guise of being helpful, initiated movements to capitalize on the Navahos' dilemma.

In the meantime, the group of newcomers proceeded to follow the suggestions for better farming made by the government. They planted fruit trees, built homes, and sent their children to the nearby mission school. Furthermore, they attempted to organize associations which they believed could solve some

Figure 1. Fruitland farms

Figure 2. The swinging footbridge

of the economic problems besetting the community at large. For example, they formed a farm association to purchase large machinery and to help merchandise their commodities. While traditional types of co-operation collapsed and old-time residents resisted the formation of associations, the newcomers advanced toward their own goals, working for the government and in town and regarding their existence in the Project in much the same individualistic manner as did their non-Navaho neighbors.

The newcomers took particular advantage of the white man's technology to raise the level of their subsistence. They had not been forced to exchange animals for land because they had never owned livestock. For them, the land was simply a free gift. For many alumni of off-reservation schools, this was a first attempt to earn a livelihood. Those with adequate training were able to secure permanent positions as part of the canal-maintenance crew. Others managed to get temporary jobs when government funds were available or when emergency work had to be done. Such jobs enabled them to utilize their learned skills and at the same time to add to the meager income from their land assignments, which were not in fact large enough to produce commodities in quantities sufficient for the markets. Incomes from the two sources enabled them to live fairly comfortably. Without kin ties in the community, they did not have to share their surplus commodities with their less fortunate relatives. Nevertheless, they remained fearful that the older farmers would force demands upon them whenever the opportunity arose.

Their relative ostracism from the community at large and their lower status position because they had no sheep or were unfamiliar with the older Navaho ways made this group tend to become "introverted" and to look for satisfying experiences outside the Navaho pattern. Thus their orientation shifted toward non-Navaho ways, with the encouragement of government personnel. This encouragement, however, was a liability as far as their relationships with traders and other Navahos were concerned. Returned students in general were considered untrustworthy. Their "half-knowledge," to use the traders' term, made them particularly unpopular. The older Navahos shifted their hostile attitudes from the government to these newcomers, who had been identified with the government program, thus transferring hostility to a target which was immediate and yet safe. Through witchcraft, gossip, and other forms of social control the newcomers were "forced" to attend and contribute to curing rites. In this way some economic leveling took place. At the same time there was sufficient leeway within the Navaho cultural pattern so that the newcomers could, for example, plant orchards, learn to preserve foodstuff by canning, and generally practice new forms of agricultural technology.

By the start of World War II the community had thus crystallized into two groups with varying orientations, each with its own established systems of interaction with the natural and social environment, each interlocked with the other. The original farmers, continuing to perpetuate many of the old grievances, maintained their hold on the community at large, partly as a defense mechanism against a seemingly capricious government but also as a means of holding together a rapidly crumbling cultural structure. The newcomers found security in their social life by associating with others like themselves, and they continued to rely on wagework to support their wives and children. In matters of health the traditionalists, though patronizing non-Navaho doctors, sponsored curing rites as well and called upon the community to help. The newcomers, unless forced to do otherwise, took their medical problems only to doctors in town.

The children of long-time residents and of outsiders who had married into the local families found themselves caught between opposing orientations. Some saw benefits in accepting new ways but were inhibited by pressures from Navaho-oriented relatives. At the same time they saw and were constantly reminded of the social and emotional support which the Navaho cultural pattern gave them.

World War II provided the third major social upheaval in Fruitland. The period between 1943 and 1946 may be termed a period of "unfreezing." [17] During these years many younger farmers were drafted or volunteered. Others went to work in the war plants, on the railroads, and on the corporation farms. Few farmers remained on the Project. Those who went away were forced to accept alien values which, in the reservation situation, they had always been free to accept or reject.

The sudden increase in income from off-reservation employment served to re-emphasize the Navahos' dependence on a wider economic structure and made them aware of the significance of education for their children, who would eventually enter into economic competition. The desire to have their children educated was, however, yet to be translated into actually sending them to school.

In their own experience, the need for education had been forcefully brought home. Men with bilingual ability were chosen as foremen or for other tasks which required less physical labor but commanded higher wages than day labor. With the termination of the war those who spoke English were again the men most often hired by the government. Now the economic and social assets of such jobs, in the context of the postwar situation, far outweighed the latent hostilities held by old residents toward Navahos who worked for the government. The newcomers' status was higher, not only because they were

[17] Kurt Lewin, "Frontiers in Group Dynamics," *Human Relations*, I (1947), 2-38.

war veterans but also because they had grown older. Moreover, many old residents were engaged in off-reservation wagework and were on the Project only during the growing season.

Those who spoke no English were now ambivalent in their attitudes toward government jobs. This was in contrast to the early 1930's when, upon learning that their jobs on the canal were not permanent, they had focused their hostility upon those who continued working. Now they too needed and liked cash incomes and therefore continued to seek work. Nevertheless, whenever the situation between the government agents and the farmers became particularly tense, those who spoke no English identified Navahos holding government jobs as "government Indians."

During the summer of 1949, when the relationship between Agency and Navahos was calm, the Tribal Council delegate from Unit 1 and others who spoke no English sought and obtained government employment. In addition, individuals living in Unit 2 also worked for the government on a part-time basis and otherwise had business transactions with the Agency. The economic values held by non-Navahos were being widely accepted. Thus the growing economic burden placed on the delegate from Unit 1 by the increased number in his family, the tuition and clothing needs of his children attending various schools, and his desire to obtain agricultural implements, all motivated him to obtain employment with the Agency in spite of possible effects on his position as delegate. In his unit at least, where the prestige system surrounding horses and livestock had become tenuous, higher status seemed to go now to those who used modern technology in their farming.

As a result of the "unfreezing" process, a new social organization developed. Although many of the old attitudes remained, they were reinterpreted or were subject to re-emphasis by the old farmers. Newcomers who before the war were considered intruders, and therefore a source of stress to the existing social organization, achieved new status. They were still considered outsiders, but they were themselves older, and they had established a closely knit society of their own, non-Navaho in pattern.

Taking 1950 as a base line, one may distinguish four different areas of compromise and conflict in the background of the Fruitland Navahos. The basic means and methods by which they secured subsistence had undergone a series of changes, some abrupt, some gradual, over a period of years. Their relations with the white communities surrounding them had also been marked by a number of shifts and alterations. Both these areas of social change had produced notable cleavages and conflicts within the ranks of the Fruitland Navaho society itself. Finally, relations with the American national government—Washington and its local representative, the Agency—had produced a history of conflict, disagreement, and social acrimony, so complex and profound as to influence radically the workings of the Fruitland culture. The next four chapters will be devoted to detailed analyses of these areas, viewed as a background for the social explosion of 1950–1952.

CHAPTER II

Agricultural Practice
and Produce

BY and large, the Fruitland farmer of 1950 did not support himself on his land. This failure resulted from more complex causes than the small size of holdings.[1] Crop yields were low, far lower than those of non-Navaho farmers across the San Juan.[2] Along with their mistrust of government personnel and government-taught methods, the Fruitlanders had been hampered by some of their own agricultural concepts, by fear of witchcraft, by the time given in summer to ceremonial activity, and sometimes by lack of any real opportunity to learn.

A few Fruitlanders, to be sure, applied poisoned bran to their fields and sprayed with chlordane as control measures against grasshoppers. Others dug their own drainage ditches to reclaim parts of their waterlogged land. A few applied sheep manure to their alfalfa fields. These isolated instances of improved farming

[1] See Table 1, page 44, for acreage of the 188 assignments.
[2] Even as late as 1951 improved corn averaged 29 bushels per acre. Native varieties averaged 18 bushels. Through crop rotation, a few farmers obtained 40 to 50 bushels per acre of the hybrid variety and up to 40 bushels per acre of the native corn.

practices were emulated to some extent by others, but it was "all up to them." If the individual were interested and had the funds and the manpower to invest, he might accept a new practice; otherwise he might decide that the old established ways were satisfactory.

Asked in 1949 about their agricultural practices, many Fruit-landers expressed instead their thoughts about non-Navaho techniques used across the river. A number of informants claimed that they used manure on their alfalfa fields when they actually did not. Again, some talked about the effectiveness of poisoned bran but did not actually apply it. Many more spoke of how they were going to improve their land at some later time. There was substantial evidence that Navahos were in-fluenced toward improved practices by non-Navaho neighbors. They listened to comments at the trading posts and related them to others in the community. Occasionally a farmer would try something new; for example, the tribal delegate hired a non-Navaho farmer to spray his beans, was able to control beetles, and realized the largest yield in San Juan County. As one Fruitlander remarked of the delegate, "He does pretty good at farming because he doesn't go away to work; he takes care of his farm." When absent himself, he left one of his two mature sons to do the farm work. His neighbors understood his ex-ample, but by and large they did not follow it.

The Navahos' perception of farming methods as carried on by their neighbors accounted for some slow improvement. But there was insufficient Indian Service personnel to direct the Navahos in advancement of their farming techniques. Before 1949 there had been two extension agents on the Fruitland Project, one for two years, the other for a much shorter period; from 1945 to 1949 there was no extension agent on the Project.

Navaho farmers working across the river observed new techniques with considerable interest, followed instructions, and saw the results. Returning to their own farms and attempting to apply like techniques of planting, they found that they had forgotten whether the rows were supposed to be eighteen or twenty-four inches apart, whether a mechanical planter should place seeds six inches or a foot apart, and whether fertilizer should be applied once or several times during the season and in what quantities.

Ritual directly associated with agriculture was no longer widely practiced at Fruitland. Although a few of the older farmers still believed that certain types of ceremonial sings served to rid the field of insects, other farmers—quite apart from the difficulty of arranging for use of the one government-owned sprayer and their own lack of cash to buy spraying compounds—simply believed that nothing could be done about insects, and so lost their crops. But the time spent on other sorts of ceremonial disrupted agriculture. One ceremony kept all the members of three family units away from their farming for four days and five nights—the patient's immediate family, members of the extended family, and clan groups were required to participate.[3] And when squaw dances were held at Shiprock, Red Rock, or Sanostee, groups of families left for several days or even a week at a time, depending on the distance they had to travel. Some few farmers traveled from one squaw dance to another, disregarding their farms entirely. Some also attended fiestas and fairs in both New Mexico and Colorado.

Necessary cutting or baling of alfalfa was left undone because helpers were not available. Some who attended cere-

[3] Kluckhohn and Leighton estimate in *The Navaho*, p. 160, that in the Ramah Navaho area the amount of time spent by Navahos on ceremonials either as patients or as helpers is one-third to one-fourth of the productive time for adult men and one-fifth to one-sixth for women. They point out (p. 162) that "a rite calls into action the immediate social organization around the patient. To carry it out properly, the help of many persons is needed: to pay the Singer and his assistants; to gather the plants and other materials; and to carry on the subsidiary activities of preparing food, maintaining the fire or fires, and providing water. The whole system is, of course, founded upon expected reciprocities."

monials made a pretense of working but did more harm than good. For example, a farmer would set the irrigation canal gates so that he could catch up on last night's sleep. When other farmers adjusted their own lateral gates, the napping farmer's crops might be washed away. On a lateral serving fifteen families, rotation of water usage could not be organized because one farmer might miss his turn if his day happened to coincide with a ceremonial. Not only were agricultural chores neglected, but expenses involved in attending ceremonials were so great as to handicap farmers in their routine endeavors and in their efforts toward emulating non-Navaho technology. Modern transportation as well as availability of alcohol only increased the expenses. At one squaw dance, men were hired to patrol the area to keep the drunks from falling into the hands of the Navaho police, and four medicine men were hired from Crystal, New Mexico; an expensive added feature was a "Mud Dance." [4]

Although sheep and dry farming constituted the Navahos' main sources of subsistence until the 1930's, when the government initiated the program of livestock reduction, irrigation farming in the Fruitland area began long before the non-Navahos settled in the valley. The first ditches were small, and only six or seven family groups had farms. Mormons, and later the government, helped the Navahos construct larger canals so that many more farmers could have irrigated tracts of land. In Unit 1 a small ditch system was dug during the mid-1920's under the supervision of Sophus Jensen, a government farm agent from Shiprock. A separate ditch system in Unit 2 was said to have been constructed under the supervision of a Mormon bishop and a trader named Curley. Hill reported in the early 1930's:

[4] This is a ceremony which occurs occasionally in connection with the "Enemy Way"; see Gladys Reichard, *Social Life of the Navajo Indian with Some Attention to Minor Ceremonies* (Columbia University Contributions to Anthropology, vol. VII; New York: Columbia University Press, 1928), pp. 132–133.

Along the San Juan River there are ditches leading from the river to the fields. The arroyos were also dammed so that the water was forced to spread over the fields. The river ditches were used only once or twice during the summer. The people irrigated from the side creeks after every flood. Most of them simply planted along the river and depended on side creeks for water. The dam and ditches were about two and one half feet high and deep respectively. Crop failures were known to have occurred from drought, but they were very rare.[5]

With respect to water usage, "water was also used communally. . . . Where ditch irrigation was practiced, the person farthest upstream used what water he wanted and those below got what was left." Once a site for a field was selected and cleared, the land was "owned" in the sense that it was being used. Land could be cultivated by anyone if it was not being farmed by the nominal owner, and until recently land had not been bought, sold, or rented. (Hill believes the reason to be that there had always been sufficient land to satisfy the demand.) In recent years pressures for available land had increased considerably, and Anglo-American patterns of selling the use of land were common.[6]

In addition to communal use of water a generation ago, planting, cultivating, and harvesting of crops called for reciprocal exchange of labor. At planting time Navahos called on all community members to come to a designated field on a certain day. No particular relatives were called; meals were the only compensation, but the recipient must reciprocate when his neighbors in turn planted. The farmers considered that products from their fields belonged to everyone in the family who had helped. It was customary, also, for wealthy individuals

[5] W. W. Hill, *The Agricultural and Hunting Methods of the Navaho Indians* (Yale University Publications in Anthropology, no. 18; New Haven: Yale University Press, 1938), p. 25.

[6] *Ibid.*, p. 21.

to share their surplus field crops and other food supplies with needy relatives and neighbors.[7]

After World War II, by contrast, Navaho farmers tended to be individualistic in their farming practices as well as in the disposition of their harvested crops. Work exchange continued among relatives, but Navahos outside the extended-family group expected pay as well as food for their labor. Furthermore, the Navahos began to select those neighbors for whom they would work, basing their choice on the quality of meal served and on the difficulty of the job.

Farmers now sold surplus crops to traders. With the cash received, they paid their old debts but avoided any traditional obligations to indigent relatives. Whereas stored hay or corn can be seen and must be shared upon request, the farmer with cash need only point to his empty crib and corral to discourage even his most insistent relatives.

The old relationship with traders, too, began to change. Traders no longer gave credit freely when they observed that a customer's sheep were being "mortgaged" to several stores or when they knew that an Indian spent his cash in town. "When they are broke, they come to the trading post."

Fruitland's two chapter farm associations, made up of people who had known each other for years, collapsed not long after the new canal was dug. Each of these earlier chapter organizations had kept a set of implements, including cultivators, planters, and a hay baler, at the yard of an officer, to be borrowed and returned by members as the need arose. When the new canal was completed, the two chapters were combined, and the communally owned implements were put to a wider use. But long-time residents resisted new neighbors' use of their implements. As late as 1949, members of the old associations still complained that many new farmers were ruining the already-worn and rusted community implements and wanted to restrict

[7] *Ibid.*, pp. 22-23.

their use to the original members who had worked to get them.

The advocates of new farm associations, young "progressive" Navahos trained at off-reservation schools, knew that only through organization could their agricultural activities be modernized and put on a practical basis:

If we had an association we would have some money . . . because each farmer would have to put in about five dollars a year. Then a time like right now came, we could get together and pay for [grasshopper] spray and make everybody spray their farms. Even if we could get a little over half the farmers to join it would be effective. We could show the other farmers that such a scheme would work and they would want to join.

But attempts to establish new associations failed.[8] To the question why such an organization was not instituted, the reply was always, "They are just indifferent and do nothing about it." Younger men, if not really "indifferent," often exhibited fear that unpopular action might earn them accusations of witchcraft. One young Navaho entered reluctantly into traditional forms of "co-operation." He lent almost a hundred dollars to five older men because if he did not, "They will speak bad about you." In any discussion of association for group action, as in any other contexts, he spoke of witchcraft practices as a reason to move slowly.[9]

In early 1940 agency personnel proposed that a farm associa-

[8] Traditional Navaho suspicion of nonrelatives must be reckoned with; see Kluckhohn and Leighton, *The Navaho*, p. 225.

[9] Clyde Kluckhohn, in *Navaho Witchcraft* (Papers of the Peabody Museum of American Archaeology and Ethnology, Harvard University, vol. XXII, no. 2; Cambridge: The Museum, 1944), p. 48, indicates that acculturated Navahos are fearful of witches even though they have lost all faith in Navaho medicine. Evon Z. Vogt states, "We find that the belief in and fear of Navaho ghosts and witches survives even in the cases of the most acculturated veterans," in his *Navaho Veterans: A Study of Changing Values* (Papers of the Peabody Museum of American Archaeology and Ethnology, vol. XLI, no. 1; Cambridge: The Museum, 1951), p. 114.

tion be organized on the Project, and in March a set of bylaws to apply to the Fruitland Irrigation Project and Farming Members was submitted to the farmers for consideration.[10] Three elective officers, a president, a vice-president, and a secretary-treasurer, were to co-operate with Navajo Service employees on all questions concerning farm management and irrigation. Assessments at the rate of $1.00 an acre per year for water usage were to be collected by the committee in cash, farm produce, or labor. Labor was to be calculated at $2.40 per day for a man or at $4.40 if he brought a team. Members not answering emergency calls, for example, during floods, were to be assessed penalties of $2.00 per acre. Other stipulations were listed as follows:

1. Water to be conserved at all times
2. Flooding of roads and wasting of water to be referred to the Association Committee
3. No livestock to be permitted at large in the farming areas
4. Farms to have a good three-wire fence.

There are no records to indicate that the new association was in fact formed. Water-assessment fees and the stipulations were enforced by Navajo Service personnel until the spring of 1949. At that time a second committee was formed of tribal delegates and chapter officers already in office, to work with the government supervisor and the irrigation engineer.

Farming practices on the Fruitland Project in 1950 ranged from good to complete neglect. Except in rare cases traditional dry-farm "hill" techniques in planting had given way to corrugated rows. The Navahos adopted, or continued to plant, those crops which fitted into the round of their religious life and accorded with their interest in livestock. Alfalfa, a recent introduction, and corn, both the Indian and the improved variety, constituted their principal crops. These were, however, culti-

[10] Fruitland, N.Mex., March 11, 1940, "By Laws Proposed to Apply to the Fruitland Irrigation Project and Farming Members."

vated with a minimum of care, often at the expense of production. Fields were left in alfalfa (planted largely because it does not have to be turned under and replanted each year, besides giving the farmers a good cash return) long after production, quality, and hence income, dropped.

Except for three tractors, two mechanical hay balers, a bean thresher, and a number of corn planters, hay mowers, and rakes, the farming implements owned by the Fruitlanders were small and limited to those that could be hand-operated or horse-drawn. The majority of the farmers plowed and cultivated with their own implements. Few owned the machines needed for mowing and raking alfalfa; these few mowed and raked for others in return for a share of the crop. Government implements—the gas-operated sprayer and the large wheat or alfalfa planter, available for 25 cents an hour—were not widely used.

Many Navahos did not dispose advantageously of what crops they harvested. They sold to the traders at once rather than storing until prices should rise; they demanded cash payment when exchange with a neighbor or payment in labor would have profited all. As in every aspect of their farming, the problem was not only introducing new techniques, but encouraging those already familiar with them.

Interest in farming was high during the planting season, but as spring and summer arrived less and less attention was paid to the growing plants. In late March and early April the farmers as a rule began to return to the Project from wagework or from their winter homes. Thereafter they prepared their fields and equipment and helped to clean the irrigation ditches, thus paying their water-assessment fees. When ditch cleaning was over, they drew water, once or more, on fields to be planted in corn or beans (for easier plowing and for two months' moisture in the ground) or already in alfalfa (for a good first cutting). Although some individual farmers continued systematic irrigation, more were slipshod, with resulting damage to the soil.

In large part such actions merely indicated neglect, but in part they were based upon belief. Some stated that the heavy alkali in the fields resulted from the digging of the new canal and not from overirrigation or lack of drainage ditches, and the exposure of subsoil was attributed to heavy runoffs of torrential showers rather than to lack of water control when the farms were irrigated. Poor crops they blamed on poor land rather than on lack of care or of proper fertilization.

Some of my land is alkali. Some is too high for the ditch, and some is too rocky. I think in about thirty years this land will be no good. It will all be in alkali. Down below you can't plow because the dirt is only about six inches deep, bottom is rock. Some is clay . . . and the water doesn't soak in. The plants all die. . . . Sometimes we tried to level this land with tractors, but we can't because it sure is hard.

Fruitlanders' past experiences had much to do with these beliefs. As already observed, the farmer whose soil was impoverished could until recently move to another piece of land. When the soil became unproductive, a man merely cleared new land or moved to Unit 3 or (more recently) applied for assignments closer to the main canal. With such excess land no longer easily available, many farmers worked their farms just enough to prevent loss of their assignments, making no effort to improve the soil.

Some farmers intentionally flooded their farms. When many irrigated from the same lateral at the same time—an inefficient practice in itself, as government employees repeatedly stressed —some left their fields unattended, in the belief that a minimum of water would enter the field. When other farmers closed their ditch gates, water gushed in on the unattended land and washed away the topsoil. Small children, left to irrigate while their parents went to squaw dances or to town, sometimes allowed flooding to such an extent that roads were washed out. After such rapid irrigation, the soil dried too quickly and had to be

irrigated again. Most Fruitlanders used more water on their
farms than necessary. Some, without proper drainage, soaked
their farms which became seeped and saline. For fear of witchcraft accusation, few practiced night irrigation—though as
government employees urged, they could thus have relieved
pressure on the available water supply and arranged a more
equitable distribution.[11]

The more able farmers made sublateral ditches, through
which water passed before entering the fields, in order to get
better control of the water and to reduce the gradient enough
so that water would not flow too swiftly into the fields. These
farmers cut grooves along the banks of the sublateral ditches at
the head of each corrugated row. They then controlled the
flow of water by packing the grooved edges with grass or with
spoiled hay.

In early May the Project's farmers were busy plowing, ir-
rigating, and harrowing, and in early June—though some waited
until late July—they planted corn and then beans. Although
most farmers plowed with their own horse-drawn walking
plows, a few hired one of the two Fruitland tractor operators.
Those who could used one of several horse-drawn planters;
others used small, hand-operated planters. For alfalfa, the
government planter was available; but more often farmers
broadcasted by hand. After plowing that part of the field to be
planted in corn or beans, the farmers cut their first stand of
alfalfa. They saved much of this first cutting for their farm
horses but baled and sold later cuttings to traders.

[11] As Kluckhohn observes in his *Navaho Witchcraft*, p. 64, "One of the
principal sources of friction among Navahos is sexual jealousy. Fear of
witches at night acts to some slight extent as a deterrent to extra-marital
sex relations because the darkness would otherwise provide favorable
conditions for a secret rendezvous." Where living is close, as it is at Fruitland, Navahos feel that nature will eventually take its course and that
sexual intercourse will occur. See Dorothea C. Leighton and Clyde Kluckhohn, *The Children of the People* (Cambridge: Harvard University Press,
1947), p. 87, and Kluckhohn and Leighton, *The Navaho*, p. 234.

Once the seed was in the ground, Fruitlanders did no more farm work until plants came up. Only then could they make the corrugated rows for irrigation. Cultivation and weeding continued haphazardly throughout the summer, usually with horse-drawn cultivators (of which all but two were the walking type). On many farms, weeds were allowed to reach two or three feet before they were cut; on more than a few, weeding was neglected altogether, and the planted crops could not be seen because of weeds.

Most farmers and their families hoed their own fields. Where an extended family lived nearby, reciprocal exchange of labor was still common, but the farmer who had to hire labor paid wages comparable to those across the river—$5 a day each, for example, to six people for four days, to hoe eight acres of corn (in addition to several head of sheep which were butchered for food, a case of bottled soda water, and watermelon). A farmer who offered $20 for hoeing his five acres had to do the work himself.

The more advanced farmers took some measures against insects and other pests. Some dug around the plants for cutworms; some picked squash bugs off the plants. One farmer applied moth balls around his squash plants, on the theory that the insects do not like the odor. About one-fourth of those growing beans borrowed the government sprayer, hired non-Navahos to spray, or used the hand-pump type of sprayers; the vast majority did nothing.

Grasshoppers were so numerous during 1949 that over half the crop in Unit 3 was damaged. Government attempts to curtail the ravages by issuing poisoned bran were ineffective. A meeting to discuss use of the poison was well attended; both Indian Service agents and the tribal delegates tried to get full co-operation of the farmers; several government trucks hauled in poison from Shiprock; and the poison, properly applied, gave noticeable relief from grasshoppers. But very few farmers used

it. Some Fruitlanders said, "Being mean to them will cause the
grasshoppers to return next year in greater numbers." Most of
the fields were severely damaged.

The trader suggested chlordane or toxaphene sprays, effective insecticides widely used. Government agents did not
recommend their use by Navaho farmers, lest stock wander into
sprayed fields, become poisoned, and endanger those who ate
their flesh. In spite of warnings, some farmers used this type
of spray.

A few older Navahos still practiced traditional methods of
pest control. A seventy-year-old farmer, for example, told how
he had applied ashes around and under the leaves of his squash
plants to keep insects away. Some bold practitioners claimed
that by ceremonial singing over their fields they had prevented
damage and suggested that others do the same. Others were reluctant to speak about their chants because they were afraid of
ridicule. Of the twenty-five farmers who were asked if they
had used chants to ward off insects and pests, only one admitted
openly that he had. Three persons told the interpreter that they
had tried them but were ashamed to talk about the practice because they were afraid of being ridiculed not only by the research worker but by other Fruitland Navahos. The research
worker was then told by the interpreter that for purposes of
controlling insects chants were now used only in the remote
parts of the reservation.

In 1942, money was collected to bring a Hopi medicine man
to perform a sing for both the Shiprock and Fruitland farming
communities. In 1949 another sing was held by a man from
Jemez Pueblo, but this time secretly and only in Unit 2, at the
urging of older farmers. By the time the sing was held, grasshoppers had already done great damage. Many farmers left for
off-reservation work immediately afterward, in the belief that
the situation was hopeless; in their years of dry farming and

floodwater farming, they observed, grasshoppers had come but rarely.

In September and early October, just before their own harvest time, many Fruitlanders left for the bean harvest in Cortez and Fort Lewis, Colorado. In 1949 only about two dozen of some two hundred persons remained in Unit 2. By the first week in October most had returned to attend the Navaho fair held at Shiprock. Their harvest was completed by November 1. Soon after they again dispersed for off-reservation work or to their winter homes on the plateau.

In 1942 Navaho farmers on the Fruitland Project realized a gross of $29.85 per acre, as against $128 per acre for non-Navahos under like soil and climatic conditions.[12] More recent figures for white farmers across the river are lacking, but production of Navaho farms can be compared with those operated by the government school in terms of specific crops for 1948. The yield per acre of improved corn from the school fields averaged 46.7 bushels and from Navaho fields less than 25, with a range between 10 and 40.[13]

From 1940 to 1949 there was a steady increase in gross value of all crops (except wheat) grown on the Project, but it was due more to rising prices and to increased acreage than to increased production per acre. Besides, the increase, from $29.85 per acre in 1942 to $54.20 in 1947, was offset by rising prices for other items.

Even without the help of a farm agent, some diversification of crops has been accomplished. Between 1940 and 1948 acreage planted in alfalfa was increased more than in any other crop, in part to augment the nitrogen content in the soil before other crops were planted and in part because alfalfa did not require

[12] Elizabeth Clark, *Report on the Navaho* (mimeographed; Washington: U.S. Indian Service, 1946).

[13] "U.S. Government Crop Reports," Fruitland Project, 1948.

heavy investments in implements. Corn also maintained a high level except for 1944, when many farmers were away at war work. Acreage in beans expanded at a rapid pace, perhaps as those working in the bean fields of Colorado became familiar with additional techniques.

Government crop records showed roughly equal value for field corn and alfalfa until 1948, when the gross value of alfalfa was twice that of corn. Other field crops such as potatoes, corn fodder, beans, squash, and melons yielded a little more than one-fourth of the gross value of alfalfa.

During the same period a greater number of farmers planted improved corn. This corn consistently yielded ten or more bushels per acre than Indian corn. Furthermore, Fruitlanders observed that improved corn could be left on the stalks to dry and then shelled immediately, whereas Indian corn had to be picked, stored, and allowed to dry before shelling. Thus, improved corn had the advantage of immediate availability for the market without the long wait required by the Indian variety. On the other hand, the difference in yields between the two varieties and the ease of harvesting are offset somewhat by the higher prices that traders pay for the Indian corn.

Vegetable gardens were small, and returns were limited accordingly. In most years after 1940 some fifteen farmers put a total of three or four acres into vegetables. In 1944, thirty-one farmers put 11.5 acres into gardens at the urging of an especially interested extension agent who was to leave the next year.

Approximately ten acres on the Project were planted in fruit trees, peaches, apricots, and apples, most of them in Unit 1. In 1948 the gross value placed on fruits was $2,455; these were either consumed fresh or canned for future consumption.

Sheep husbandry was the primary source of income for a few farmers and a supplementary source of income for others. Of the total of 191 farm operators in 1948–1949, there were 82, or well less than half, who owned sheep. Of these, 24 had more sheep than their Indian Service permits allowed them, and 52 had less. (Two farmers held permits but owned no sheep.) These permits, based upon the carrying capacity of the range and on the number of sheep owned by the individual when the stock-reduction program was instituted in the early 1930's, represented a reduction of all herds "across the board." But the number of sheep allowed most families was not large enough so that natural reproduction would maintain the flocks. Each season sickness, accidents, and slaughtering for food reduced the size of flocks, until small owners could afford neither the money nor the time to care for so few animals adequately. Some sold their permits to larger operators, and still others with small flocks held on to them because "some day we might be able to fill it up again." Only 17 owned enough sheep to make cash profits,[14] one more than 300, the rest between 100 and 250. Other owners used the animals for food and the wool for rug weaving. Some 45 of these owned between 51 and 100 sheep units, and the rest less than 50.

Only 33 per cent of the farmers in the largest unit, Unit 1, owned sheep; 80 per cent in Unit 2 owned sheep; and 50 per cent in Unit 3. Despite government efforts to assign land to families without sheep, the stockowners held more acreage than those who had no stock. The stockmen-farmers who owned 50 or less head of sheep had an average landholding of 10 acres. Those who owned between 51 and 250 sheep averaged 13 acres. The individual who owned more than 300 head had 17 acres. Except for horses classified as farm horses, all the livestock fed on tribally owned range, not on irrigated land.

[14] The U.S. Department of the Interior (*The Colorado River*, A Comprehensive Departmental Report on the Development of the Water Resources for Review Prior to Submission to Congress, 1945, p. 266) reveals that at least 400 sheep per family are required to provide a minimum standard of living.

CHAPTER III

Red Man and White

NAVAHOS as a group have been treated differently from whites. The penalty for drunkenness in Farmington has always been more severe for Navahos than for non-Indians. The Navahos as a whole have been considered inferior human beings, with "more illegitimate children than any other group of people in the United States." Their dress, their language, the outlying section of town where they gathered, all have militated against them. The few "educated" Indians, holding jobs in garages, trading posts, laundries, and restaurants, have apparently won respect. The "half-educated" Navahos, however, have been considered "smart alecks," "no-goods." The uneducated were "just plain ignorant," but at least they were said to keep their word and, in general, to be more trustworthy than the others. These attitudes were not only the general attitudes held among the white population around the Fruitland area; they were largely shared by traders and by Indian Service personnel, the success of whose work depended entirely upon the Navahos.

Ignorance and misunderstanding were not, of course, unilateral. Fruitland Navahos traditionally had economic relations only with restricted categories of non-Navahos—merchants, missionaries, and civil servants. Thus their image of the white world was narrow and biased. They experienced separately types of white behavior and white beliefs which were rarely congruent with one another; and they were hardly in a position to form a fair judgment of the society as a whole.

Yet Fruitland Navahos had been in contact with the outside world since 1876, when Farmington was first settled. In the very next year the village now known as Fruitland was established by Mormons led by Luther E. Burnhams.[1] A government boarding school for Navaho children was built between 1900 and 1905 at Shiprock. The superintendent of the area, a man of strong character and great determination, bent his energies to eradicate Navaho ways of life as quickly as possible and by any means which he thought effective.[2] Many local Navahos attended this school and others located in California, Oklahoma, Kansas, Colorado, and Pennsylvania. Resentful of the scorn for Indian ways they often encountered at the schools, they returned to Fruitland to become bitter critics of Indian Service policies. On the "rebound," they submerged themselves more deeply in their own culture. Their and their neighbors' visits to town were infrequent. Usually, because of the cost, only male members of families went to town. Women and children went when they needed treatment at the clinic or at the mission hospital.

Criticism of federal policies was especially bitter after the middle 1930's. The stock-reduction program caused a storm of antiwhite manifestations which continued for years. As one non-Navaho remembered, "When the stock-reduction came

[1] Writers' Program of the Work Projects Administration, *New Mexico: A Guide to the Colorful State* (New York: Hastings House, 1940), p. 363.
[2] Leighton and Kluckhohn, *Children of the People*, p. 125.

. . . hundreds of sheep were burned on the empty lot near the Fruitland Trading Company. Only the pelts were left for the Navahos, and $1.00 a head. It was a pitiful sight." And as a Fruitlander put it, "The Navahos were ordered to reduce their flock to a particular size immediately, and if they didn't do it, the police came out, rounded up the sheep and slaughtered the animals. Some of The People were so mad they quit herding sheep entirely."

At this time too the Fruitlanders came under the influence of a few non-Navaho agitators and began to quarrel with the government on various issues. A Navaho from Farmington organized the Navajo Progressive League as a reaction to stock reduction and drew into it fellow tribesmen from all over the reservation. The traders, although interested in the welfare of the Navahos, added to the existing confusion. They saw the livelihood of the Navaho disappear with what at least seemed the indiscriminate killing of sheep and goats. To them as to many others the long-range program of soil conservation meant little; and even if some saw its benefits theoretically, they, like the Navahos, could not accept stock reduction calmly. In this psychological and social atmosphere, the Fruitland Project emerged.

The idea for an Irrigation Project at Fruitland first developed during the 1920's. It did not progress beyond the planning stages until funds became available under the Work Projects Administration in the 1930's. Its purpose was to provide a new subsistence base for a few hundred families. The consequences were unexpected. The Project was a major engineering feat, and its technical aspects were well planned and executed. Theoretically, the Navahos could have benefited. Unfortunately, the administrators were inadequate. They upset the existing social organization by bringing in outsiders, by leveling the people economically, and by urging livestock men to give up their herds in exchange for farms. Worst of all, they later reversed their own land policy—to effect another reduction, this time in acreage.

There was, in addition, one radical inconsistency within the original program itself. For although the aim was subsistence farming, the planners inadvertently encouraged the assignees to become part-time commercial farmers. Urging the Navahos to plant legumes such as alfalfa in order to check erosion and build up the soil and later stressing crop rotation, they effected a division of the ten-acre "subsistence" farms into two fields, one in alfalfa and the other in native corn, beans, squash, and melons. Now farmers neither raised enough food crops to store for the winter nor produced enough alfalfa to sell for cash. Although some farmers could eke out a living from their sheep, most had from the beginning to rely on welfare agencies or wagework.[3]

---

[3] *Types of Farming and Ranching Areas in New Mexico* (Bulletin 267; State College: New Mexico College of Agriculture and Mechanic Arts, May, 1939), II, 130–131, designates the location of non-Indians' farms directly across the San Juan River as Sub-area 25-B and includes the communities of Waterflow, Fruitland, and Kirtland. The most important types of farming are crop specialties (alfalfa) and general farming, which types make up 29 and 21 per cent respectively of the total number. Crop-specialty farms in 1939 had an average of approximately 42 acres each. The general farms, comprising a variety of agricultural enterprises such as alfalfa, corn, beans, hogs, dairying, fruit, and vegetables, averaged approximately 26 acres. Part-time and self-sufficing farms made up 13 and 8 per cent respectively of the total number, but were considered of little importance as commercial farms because of their limited size; the part-time farms averaged 5 acres, and the self-sufficing farms harvested an average of 13 acres.

Thus in many ways the Navaho farms resembled the specialty farms across the river. For purposes of retarding erosion the planting of cover crops was urged. Furthermore, the Navahos were reminded that alfalfa had brought in more cash than corn or other crops (Minutes of the Community Meeting, April 4, 1941). Unwittingly, it seems that the government was asking the Navahos to take up white farming ways, but not white values regarding the profit motive. Navaho awareness of such a contradiction was not lacking, as noted in their comments.

In October, 1933, the survey work for the irrigated tracts began [4] in three areas where a number of Navahos already farmed and raised livestock. The government first announced that each family unit was to receive twenty acres of land.[5] The Navahos also understood that permanent government jobs would be available to families complying with the livestock-reduction program. A tribal delegate said later:

Back in 1937, some kind of party came here and told me if I got rid of 50 head of sheep they'd give me a job for five years. The job lasted me only six months. That happened to a lot of stockmen. . . . After that they rustled me another job which I never got. People became afraid of taking new programs.

To be sure, when the major task of digging the canal began, many Fruitlanders were recruited as laborers, along with other Navahos, mostly students returned from off-reservation schools. But when farms became available, the government announced that plots were to be smaller than twenty acres.[6] The land would be assigned to Navahos from other areas as well as to Fruit-landers. Preference in assignment was given to those who had no livestock. Thus, the policy of establishing Fruitland as an Irrigation Project was essentially that of giving aid to Navahos with no other means of livelihood; the small plots of land assigned to individual family units were to be used as subsistence farms rather than operated for profit. (Since the land is

[4] *Farmington Times Hustler,* Oct. 20, 1933. The area was first surveyed as a possible site for an irrigation project twelve years before, according to the April 14, 1921, copy of the same newspaper.

[5] "It is planned to move approximately 255 families to this tract. It is proposed to subdivide the entire area into small irrigable plots of 20 acres each" (*Farmington Times Hustler,* July 20, 1934, p. 1).

[6] *Farmington Times Hustler* (April 24, 1936) reported, "Little if any actual farming will be done under the Fruitland Project this year despite the fact water has been in the canal for several weeks. This is due to cancellation of the original 20-acre allotments, many of which had even been fenced, and the substitution of the plan of ten-acre tracts."

tribally owned, there would be no tax assessments or rental charges.)

The Fruitlanders felt this to be a breach of faith. In meeting after meeting they asked for renewal of the twenty-acre assignments, refused to give up their livestock, and demanded first consideration in the selection of land. The superintendent of the Navajo Reservation urged, in a meeting at Fruitland in April, 1938:

There are a number of Navahos here and elsewhere who do not own sheep. The Fruitland Project and other projects are planned to help all the Navahos, but specifically the Navahos who do not own any sheep or livestock, and last chance must be given to people who own sheep and are now using Navaho resources in the form of grass. [Land distribution] should be confined to the people and the returned students who don't have sheep and should have a chance to earn a living on this land.[7]

In response, a native Fruitlander said, "He mentioned those that didn't have sheep, and didn't have land. Of course, some of us are thrifty and have more and more, and we think we should get as much as we can. There are a lot of poor Navahos, but naturally, it's their own fault they haven't got anything."

At the same meeting another government spokesman stated:

We have been debating about the size of farm a Navaho should have. I wonder if he really knows how much is ten acres or nineteen acres of land. Each year we make a careful survey of each irrigation project on the Reservation to make a crop report to Washington of the crops that are grown. We keep a careful record of the amount of crops from the land. Almost invariably a man who has five to ten acres has more crops than a man who has twenty, thirty, or forty acres. What's the use of arguing about a piece of land when you can make more out of a smaller farm than if you have more land? This is actually being done by the Navahos on the Reservation.

[7] Minutes of the Community Meeting, Fruitland, N. Mex., April 14, 1938.

In response, one tribal delegate said:

I know the size of a ten acre farm and I know one acre, five acres. The reason we are asking for more than ten acres is that we have seen and experienced farming. Take a large farm and you cultivate it for a number of years, and run water on it. There's a certain percentage of that land where alkali will form.[8] Naturally that part wouldn't be any good. . . . That's the reason we are asking for more. I have land down along the river, and six acres of that land is just lying idle because I can't raise anything on it.[9]

Although the force of these arguments was not overlooked by government officials, it seemed to them that the prospective land assignees were being incited to rebel by outsiders, as well as by their own people. A memorandum issued three weeks after the April meeting stated:

Definitely the feeling was that not even if the 10-acre assignment had been cleared up, as it could have been, no reconciliation could have been effected. Between Thursday and Monday some trouble-making

[8] This phenomenon has been observed on the farms across the river by the New Mexico Agricultural Experiment Station (*Types of Farming and Ranching Areas in New Mexico*, II, 133): "A considerable acreage of land is seeped and in a highly saline condition. In the river bottom land this may be attributable to irrigation without adequate drainage over a period of years. It is thought that seepage and salinity on the slopes have been caused by seepage from the main canals and also by the application of too much water to the land." During the summer of 1948 one Fruitland Navaho made this comment: "Since the siphon was put in, the water from the upper ditch has seeped down and carried alkali to my old farm so that it is not so good now."

[9] This statement appears to the writer to be significant. Prior to the establishment of the Fruitland Project the people could by hard work subjugate new fields when their old fields became useless. When the government took over the Project, land had become scarce and new plots were to be assigned by the agency office. Thus, as security, the Navahos demanded twenty acres whether they could farm it or not. The same reasoning applies to their desire for livestock. Navahos wished to keep more than their permitted number because sickness, lack of feed, and so on could strike when least expected.

individual had apparently sown new seeds of discontent with a view to preventing an amicable settlement.[10]

In any event, reconciliation was not effected. As a farmer said later:

Before they finished the ditch they told me I could get twenty acres if I worked it. So I got down there, put up posts, and fenced it around—then I put the water through. I had 100 sheep and I sold them because I thought I could have a big farm. When I got through plowing ten acres I heard they were going to give me just ten acres. I just quit. They promised it, and I got mad. I was willing to take at least fifteen acres, so I went to Shiprock but they wouldn't give it to me. So from then on I just quit, and didn't bother the government any more.

In addition to their dissatisfaction over reduction in acreage the Fruitlanders were concerned with the provision that land not used would revert to the government for reassignment. Although the provision followed fairly closely the traditional land-use concept, it was a real threat now that free land was no longer available. Another cause of insecurity was the fact that assignments were made to male heads of families rather than in the traditional pattern of inheritance through the maternal line.[11]

The settling of inheritance claims by a committee (composed of the local leaders and government agents) also seemed a threat, even though members of the family of the deceased had priority over the assignments. The Fruitlanders' real mistrust was of the government; their real fear was that the land might be taken away at any time by an arbitrary act on the part of those with power.

Meanwhile, many young returned students from other areas of the reservation made applications for land. Having no tools

[10] Memorandum to the Superintendent from the Section on Human Surveys, May 4, 1938.

[11] Kluckhohn and Leighton, *The Navahos*, p. 59.

and little experience, they realized that they could not farm
more than ten acres; furthermore, they understood the rehabilitation policy more clearly than did others. Some of them
purchased equipment on the government rehabilitation program, with the understanding that payments toward the purchases would be made over a period of years. Some also built
homes under the same agreement. By contrast, Fruitlanders
forced their younger men to reject or return farm plots of less
than twenty acres and discouraged them from accepting loans
for implements or homes. "It is just another trick by the
government," said one young Navaho. Twelve years later he
was to regret that he had been influenced by his elders.

The Navahos were told definitely in November, 1939, that
the assignments were meant to be subsistence farms. An agency
memorandum stated:

It was necessary for me to give information that had not been
brought out up to that time. This was that the appropriation for
the construction of the Fruitland Project was made for the purpose
of developing subsistence farms, and it was absolutely necessary that
we stay within the meaning of the appropriation.[12]

Because government policy regarded land assignments in
terms of subsistence, Indian Bureau personnel planned a survey
to determine the number and ages of children in each family,
the livestock owned, and income from other sources. The
Indians felt that the questions asked had nothing to do with the
assignment of land. A chapter officer remarked at a meeting in
February, 1940:

Each time some one inquired about a land assignment there are many
questions asked. . . . We don't like these questions, we want you
to give us twenty acres. . . . We think anyone who lives on this
river should have twenty acres if he asks for it.[13]

[12] Memorandum to the Superintendent from the Director of Land Use,
Dec. 1939.
[13] Minutes of the Community Meeting, Feb. 5, 1940.

By now the Navahos on the Project were rejecting the idea of subsistence farms and expressing their desire to make money from their fields.

When we were assigned twenty acres and started clearing and fencing it we were happy. Then they changed to ten and everyone gave up. . . . The white people across the river tell us that we can only starve on ten acres. That is not enough on which to raise a family.

And again,

I don't think ten acres is going to do me much good with five acres in alfalfa, some melons and corn. Not much is realized for a family of six. I believe twenty acres will be required. Then I might be able to raise a little something to sell for clothing, but I can't get anywhere with ten acres.

The government held to its basic policy of subsistence farms, but some concessions were made. At a meeting held in March, 1940, the district supervisor remarked

that the upper unit was about all issued and that there would be no changes up there except perhaps one or two where it was definitely established that more land was needed in order for a man and his wife to subsist. Some of the land was being held, so that if Mr. F. saw fit to increase the number of acres where the need was definitely established, perhaps some of this land could be given to those with large families, or who were assigned to poor land.

Although some land was issued as early as 1936, only a few farmers formalized their agreement with the government at that time. A statement by the supervisor making the land-assignment policy flexible proved acceptable to Fruitlanders. Beginning in 1940 more and more of them agreed to sign the statement which said, in effect, that the land was theirs so long as they made productive use of it. In one year forty-three heads of families received land under these conditions. However, agreement with the land-assignment policy in its new form did not necessarily imply a kindlier attitude toward the outsiders

who had suddenly become one's neighbors. Nor did it lead
immediately to the development of a social organization suit-
able for making maximum use of water or of land.

By 1948, 205 farms were assigned to 191 family units. The
size of assignments varied between 4.96 and 33.00 acres. (See
Table 1.) Fifty-two per cent of the farms were 10 acres or less;
89 per cent were 15 acres or less.

Table 1. Land assignment on the Fruitland Project

Acres	No. of family units
5 or less	6
6 to 10	93
11 to 15	50
16 to 20	29
21 to 25	7
26 to 30	2
30 or more	1
	188 *

* The records indicate that three Navahos have joint assignments with
other members of their families.

During World War II there was little agricultural activity
on the Fruitland Project. Before the community became
established, the younger Navahos (and agency personnel) volunteered or were drafted into military service. Older farmers
left also, to work in ordnance depots and mines and on railroads. Those who remained were predominantly the very old,
women with young children, and some younger men rejected
by the armed forces because of physical defects or illiteracy.

When the war ended, a gradual return to the land followed.
The government cleared more irrigable land, and as new fields
became available, they were assigned to veterans. Fruitlanders
continued to leave the reservation "to earn money" with which
to purchase farm tools and support their families. Shortage of
government personnel continued, and problems of land usage

Figure 3. Fields destroyed by grasshoppers

Figure 4. Sheep camp in a drought period

Figure 5. Pipeline work

Figure 6. Checking registration slips

and of sheep and horse reduction resulted in many clashes between the government and the Navahos.

Many Fruitland Navahos still complained about the limited size of the farms assigned to them. Some farmers had temporarily solved the limited acreage problem by leasing land from others on a share basis. On land already planted to alfalfa or in other crops, the lessee received one-half of the crop; where the entire crop was planted and cared for by the lessee, he received two-thirds. More frequently relatives appropriated farms belonging to other members of the family without change of title.

More important, Fruitlanders still feared that their land might be taken by the government without just cause; the subject was repeatedly discussed at meetings (and is an unsettled issue for many to this day). "How long [are] these assignments good to an Indian? For how many years?" one man asked the superintendent in 1938. The reply was, "Good for life, as long as beneficial use is made of them." In 1949 an elderly Fruitlander still said:

This is not our land. It belongs to the government. We don't know how much we should put into the farm because we don't know when the government is going to take the land away from us. It is just like what they did with our sheep. The gave them to us, but they took it away too.

Wagework also, over the years, involved difficult adjustments. Opportunities for wagework away from the reservation existed from the time of the first Mormon settlement along the river and the building of the Denver and Rio Grande Railroad's narrow-gauge tracks. Many years ago a few Indians went as far as Kansas and Oklahoma for farm employment. The Work Projects Administration and the Civilian Conservation Corps of the 1930's, however, gave a majority of Fruitlanders their first long period of work for pay. Most held off-reservation jobs during the war, and increasingly thereafter. In the late thirties they had suffered through the winters when their crops had been damaged by drought or by pests. Now the majority left for off-reservation employment immediately after their work in the fields was completed; some even departed in the slack period of the growing season at the risk of crop failure.[14] Most worked for the large corporation farms that have been established at Bluewater, New Mexico; Cortez and Fort Lewis, Colorado; and Phoenix, Arizona. The railroads employed the next largest number, although living conditions precluded the workers' being accompanied by their families. A few worked in Colorado mines. Those with special skills secured employment on the periphery of the reservation, where their abilities as stone masons or carpenters were in demand.

Incomes from off-reservation work varied. Several miners reported weekly incomes of $135, on a contract basis, but usually Navaho miners earned between $60 and $70. Work in the mines was steady, and Navaho miners were able to purchase cars and pickup trucks. Farm employment probably netted the individual the least, but family members, working together at their own pace, occasionally made as much as $60 or $70 a week.[15] The work was, however, seasonal and highly irregular because of weather conditions. At Phoenix in the winter of 1948–1949 much time was lost because of unseasonal rains.

Although work in the bean fields in Colorado was of short duration, individual Navahos were able to earn between $40 and $50 a week. The required stacking of pulled bean plants into small piles was light enough to be participated in by women and by boys of thirteen and fourteen. Thus, when family

[14] The eight family heads remaining in Unit 2 in Dec., 1949, either held steady local jobs (four with the government, one in Farmington) or were old.

[15] Kluckhohn and Leighton (*The Navaho*, p. 24) state that in 1944 "Navahos earned $785,000 in planting, weeding, and harvesting irrigated crops at Bluewater, New Mexico."

groups worked together, their earnings for the short period were very lucrative.

Railroad laborers earned 97½ cents an hour, with two extra cash benefits: time and a half for overtime and winter "layoff" unemployment compensation to the maximum amount of $5 a day for ten days out of every fourteen.[16] The traders commonly recruited their Navaho customers as railroad laborers; one trader reported that, of the 28 Fruitlanders he recruited in 1947, 15 worked less than four months, 8 between five and eight months, and 5 worked between nine months and a year. Table 2 indicates their net earnings, after deduction of with-

Table 2. Net income of 28 Fruitland Navahos employed by railroad companies in 1947 *

Income	No. of Navahos
$ 1–$ 200	4
201– 400	6
401– 600	5
601– 800	4
801– 1,100	2
1,001– 1,500	4
1,501– 2,000	2
2,001– 2,500	1
	28

* From data supplied by a local trader.

holding tax and unemployment contributions (it is not clear from the data whether subsistence is also deducted). For several men net income was less than $90 a month; the largest

[16] The daily unemployment benefit rate varies with the amount of money each worker received during the previous year. The minimum daily benefit is $1.75 for the unemployed railroad worker who has earned between $150.00 and $199.99 during the previous twelve months. The daily benefit increases as the earnings for the previous year go up. The maximum daily benefit of $5.00 goes to the unemployed railroad worker who has earned $2,500.00 or more the previous year.

monthly income was $198. The great majority earned about $125 a month.

Three English-speaking Fruitlanders were employed the year round by the Irrigation Project, and a number of others were hired on a temporary basis. The school furnished full-time employment for one farm wife and part-time employment for two farmers. Three Navahos without farms were on the Education Division staff; two more worked at the Shiprock Agency, one on a permanent basis with the Soil and Moisture Division and the other on a temporary basis with the building-construction program.

Subsidiary income was realized by a few male silversmiths and a large number of women engaged in rug weaving. The finished products were sold primarily to traders, but a few were purchased directly from the craftsmen by other Navahos. A few farmers, as will be seen, did some custom plowing and planting. Three farmers in Unit 2 with prior rights to coal mines nearby sold coal to people in Farmington, to the government agency, and to other Navahos. But only wagework and, in 1950, predominantly wagework away from home brought significant cash income to the Navaho for whom farming provided an inadequate livelihood. Off-reservation the Indians were confronted by alien values and by their dependence on a non-Navaho economy. Although they could make the necessary decisions—to seek work, to get their children the best possible education, and the like—adjustment was difficult. As a result, protective magic was widely invoked.

"Enemy Way" ceremonials including squaw dances were held frequently throughout the summer of 1949; their aim was primarily to dispel the evil of white contact rather than to cure the sick. Squaw dances attracted most of the people in the community, and very few Navahos could be found on their farms. Prior to the rituals, manpower and wagons were marshaled to gather cottonwood poles and branches for the ramadas, and families left their homes in the morning or the day before the event in order to arrive at the dance grounds on time. Often several ceremonies were in progress simultaneously, each lasting for three days and three nights. The days were spent in eating and in sleeping off the effects of the long nights of singing and dancing.[17]

It was believed that only Navaho rituals could alleviate such fundamental causes of disease as taboo transgression, and some ceremonies were devoted to this purpose. At least eight of the patients concerned, however, had had treatment at the white hospitals.[18]

There was a woman shaman who specialized in prophesying and diagnosing the illnesses resulting from contact with non-Navahos. She lived in Carson, ten or fifteen miles south of Fruitland, and was appealed to by many Navahos who wanted information about their sons in the armed forces. Prophesying with a small basket and a bundle of feathers (like the Jicarilla Apaches, it was said), she told them what they wanted to know.

I heard a lot about that woman, and after I came back from the war I went over to see her and I just couldn't believe it. A White man who was married to a Navaho was getting kind of worried about his son who was supposed to be missing in action. . . . I went with him, and this woman took us to a hogan and told us to sit at one side. She sat on the other side, and she had a basket with a bundle of white feathers in it. It was tied up in a bunch, all of them standing up. Then she started to sing, and it became quiet. Then I heard some voices.

[17] See Kluckhohn and Leighton, *The Navaho*, p. 157.

[18] The director of the enormously successful Episcopal Mission Hospital (one obstetrical case in 1931; 180 cases in 1948) stated that every medicine man in the vicinity had been in the hospital at least once, and he believed that many direct their patients to the hospital when they feel that cure of organic ailments is necessary. The hospital doctor (who has contributed service gratis for over two decades) and a nurse (who has served for an equal length of time) have not discouraged the use of sings but have even permitted a sing to be held just outside the hospital grounds.

I looked around the hogan to see where it came from. I couldn't see anything. The voice said that in six days the father would get a letter that would tell him that his son would be coming home in two months. After that we went to Farmington six days later to see if the letter came. It was there all right, and we found that in two months that son was coming back.

She seemingly had some knowledge of medical procedures, as evidenced in the tale of how she "prophesied" (diagnosed) for a woman from Fort Defiance:

At the hospital [there] they couldn't tell her what was wrong with her. She heard that this [medicine] woman could tell her what was wrong with people, even after the hospital couldn't tell. This woman was told that she had a hard time giving a baby and that she had an operation. This operation made it pretty hard for her whenever she was to be sick just about once a month. The blood inside of her just kept going around in circles, and it wouldn't come out. This lady told the sick woman what was wrong with her and told her to go to the hospital this side of Farmington to get another operation so that she wouldn't be sick that once a month. They gave her the operation so that the blood would come out, and she has been all right ever since then.[19]

One Fruitlander went to this shaman at Carson when his sons and a daughter—the sons, at least, affected by white contact—sickened or turned troublemakers.

In summary, the experience of the Fruitland community with their white neighbors was crucially determined by considerations of economic policy and advantage. When abrupt and radical changes of government policy threatened their livelihood, the Navahos were less likely to direct their resentments against an organization as powerful, impervious, and remote

---

[19] When the woman shaman advised one Navaho with "a cold in the head, and the cold went to his ear" to go to the doctor, he "paid the doctor $2.00 and the druggist $5.00 for the medicine; for the woman's advice he paid $1.50."

as the government. Rather, the conservative elements focused on immediate scapegoats—the Navaho "outsider" or the Navaho with a government job or the agent who was "unfriendly" to Navahos. When change was not so abrupt but more widespread, conservative anxiety took the form of revived ceremonial practices. Religious restrictions, ceremonial dances, witchcraft accusations, and countermeasures against the witchcraft practices imputed to others were powerful weapons in the defense of a way of life which seemed to be insidiously undermined from within rather than directly threatened from without.

CHAPTER IV

Social Organization within the Navaho Community

BY 1950 Navaho social organization in Fruitland was markedly different from that on most of the reservation. Many Fruitlanders still believed that traditional ways were best, though they found them difficult to maintain. But the assignment of Project acreage to strangers, the unusual closeness of one home to another, and the relative unimportance of livestock, all resulted in a mingling of traditional and new relationships, both within the family and in the three units. Different families and even different units displayed considerable variations in adjustment and in social tensions and pressures exercised.[1]

Because land assignments were made to the individual male head of the family and because only enough land was assigned to support the immediate (biological) family, lines of

[1] Since social groupings and relationships among Navahos are generally characterized by flexibility because of their informal social organization, it could be said that social groups and relationships at Fruitland had simply deviated still further from the traditional pattern.

domestic responsibility tended to concentrate on husband, wife, and children.[2]

Long ago I had to live with my wife's family. The family all lived together. They still do that way in the mountain, but here along the river, they work for themselves. Everyone goes away and makes his own living. They used to work all together, but now they go out by themselves. The people are trying to be like White people. Of course, the White people have money and they can pay by the day. But we don't have money so we have to work for ourselves. If I try to get somebody to work for me I have to pay five dollars a day. If I pay them that much they will clean me out.

Until 1950, a man's farm income was usually sufficient to cover only the barest needs of the immediate family. His contributions from wagework toward the support of his family were erratic, and he usually returned with little or no cash. In the Navaho tradition, he could and did spend his individual earnings as he pleased. He expected his wife to sell what she owned of the livestock and livestock products for the support of her children and herself.

At Fruitland the mother of the family was thus more vulnerable than under the traditional system. Relying on her own credit rating at the store to keep her family in groceries, she might depend on the trader to exert some pressure on her husband to help. (The traders urged heads of families to work for railroad companies; and although they had no direct access to pay checks, they were able to see that the family was fed when

[2] William T. Ross, in his "Navaho Kinship and Social Organization" (unpublished Ph.D. dissertation, University of Chicago, 1955), p. 23, shows that of Fruitland Navahos only 20 per cent lived with the wife's family, far less than reported for the reservation as a whole by David F. Aberle, in "Navajo Kinship: A Trial Run" (prepared for the Social Science Research Council Summer Session on Kinship, Harvard University, 1954), pp. 22–24. Of all Fruitland families, 65 per cent lived apart from either husband's or wife's kin.

unemployment checks arrived.) But she could no longer expect help from her own relatives, generally in the same situation. Neither her husband nor her brother was consistently home to share, as was traditional, in the training of children; and indeed, with the children themselves away at boarding school through the winter, the mother sometimes felt that she had little part in raising them.

The son-in-law's position had also changed. In an earlier period he spent many years working under the direction of his father-in-law, establishing his own household only as a fully mature person; now he spent little time in the hogan of his wife's family (though to do so was still considered the ideal pattern). Upon receiving a land assignment, he moved to his farm as soon as he could erect a house.

When a young man left the reservation to work, his wife had several choices: to live with her own family, to live with her husband's family, or to continue living in her own home. Whichever choice she made involved strain. Her own family did not welcome her because she added to its burden. Her husband's family did not welcome her because of the tensions which usually developed between daughter-in-law and mother-in-law. Her own home was a lonely place, particularly when she did not have children; besides, when alone, she had difficulty obtaining firewood, water, and groceries. Under the circumstances she usually moved about from one home to another; if able to speak English, she tried to get employment in town as dishwasher or maid. The father of a marriageable daughter was asked where she would live if she married. He expressed the uncertainty which characterized the family relationships:

If she stays here with me, it is up to me. But if she stays over there at Mary's Restaurant, then it is up to her. If she gets a good man, then her husband can have this farm. I plan everything for her. I can build another house, and then I can rest. Her husband can do the work. But if the husband doesn't want to live here, then it is up to him.

Nevertheless, members of an extended family worked together when they could, co-operating and participating in sings and caring for the infirm and for young children. Sometimes pressure was applied to secure reciprocity and co-operation. When an influential Fruitland farmer had his new field plowed by six teams, three clan relatives were obligated to help, and two neighbors also joined in, one so that he could get the use of a corn planter, the other lest the farmer "talk behind his back." Beliefs concerning traditional family relationships still remained strong, but the exigencies of the economic situation forced the Fruitlanders to make some adaptations. Until 1950, even though strains were becoming more numerous, the people still adhered generally to traditional patterns.

Fruitland had many of the characteristics which Kluckhohn describes as conducive to witchcraft beliefs, including especially the proximity of homes.[3] Combined with extensive group and intergroup frictions, witchcraft kept many who would normally be innovators from becoming too aggressive. Leadership was thus discouraged.[4] The most "progressive" young men, many of them residents only since receiving land assignments, were considered outsiders and thus were particularly easy targets for witchcraft gossip.[5] A certain amount of freedom existed for these newcomers in their new surroundings, just as men who worked away from the reservation or spent years in the armed service experienced freedom.[6] But the fact that they were still in Navaho country, surrounded by Navaho social environment, made them aware of the strength of witchcraft belief.

[3] These characteristics include objective hazards of the physical, biological, and social environments (Kluckhohn, *Navaho Witchcraft*, p. 50), the patrilocal residence which creates new strains on the social relationships (p. 51), the strong non-Indian pressures (p. 66), and this matter of proximity of homes (p. 55).

[4] *Ibid.*, pp. 60, 62, 63.   [5] *Ibid.*, p. 55.

[6] Evon Z. Vogt, "Between Two Worlds—Case Study of a Navaho Veteran," *The American Indian*, V (1949), 18.

Witchcraft belief tended to force the acculturated Navahos who no longer believed in curing rites to attend them and, therefore, to neglect their work.

I am called a witch because I don't believe in Navaho sings. I have been too educated, and I know that disease is spread at those sings. When somebody's got tuberculosis and they are having a sing they pass the cup around the room and everybody including the little kids take a drink of the medicine. . . . When they pass the medicine around I pass it to the next man. I tell them that I take the medicine in a spoon. They laugh and say that I am a White man. [Do they all call you anything else?] They call me a witch because I don't believe in Navaho religion.

Although Fruitlanders could avoid helping neighbors in the fields, it was almost impossible to avoid helping at a ceremonial. Three of the most "progressive"—close friends and technically trained men who earned substantial incomes—achieved recreational outlets by going to motion pictures and by working hard to improve their knowledge of machinery.[7] They assisted at curing rites only when specifically asked and even then stayed for only a few hours. Others, who had no cars or who had close family ties in the community, spent much of their time helping relatives and others at rites. They were constantly embarrassed financially, called on to donate time they might have devoted to farming, and forced to make other adaptations.[8] They resented their relatives' "borrowing," but they could not forestall it except by remaining without funds and food. Accordingly, they marketed hay as soon as it was mowed, spent lavishly on luxury items, and took recreational trips to Farmington, Durango, and Gallup.

[7] Cf. the similar pattern of "progressive" described by John Useem, Gordon Macgregor, and Ruth Useem, in their "Wartime Employment and Cultural Adjustment of the Rosebud Sioux," *Applied Anthropology,* II (1943), 7.
[8] *Ibid.*

Over a period of time a gradual shift toward non-Navaho ways of envisaging the supernatural took place. Men employed away from home could no longer devote hours recounting myths to their children during the winter. Even religious practitioners were affected. Drinking was common among the singers, and the same sanctions did not seem to be invoked against it at curing rites as prevailed in former years. Diagnosticians at Fruitland [9] also drank heavily, and this conduct could only accelerate the trend away from the old observances.

For purposes of electing delegates to the new Tribal Council, Fruitland was divided in 1938 into two "election communities," Upper Fruitland or Unit 1 and Lower Fruitland comprising Units 2 and 3.[10] When the canal was completed, the two old "chapters" were combined into one over-all local government. Officers were selected from each of the different units, and at least one person represented each; but the office of presidency was always occupied by a Navaho from Unit 2.

The main communication between the federal agency and the community was through the council delegates.[11] They were elected for four-year terms by residents of the communities in which they lived. Colored ballots were used, each candidate being identified by a color. The delegates attended Tribal Council meetings at Window Rock and participated with members from other districts on matters having to do with the tribe as a whole. "The Council passes on expenditures of tribal funds; defines conditions of tribal membership; regulates the domestic

[9] See Alexander H. and Dorothea C. Leighton, *Gregorio, the Hand Trembler* (Papers of the Peabody Museum of American Archaeology and Ethnology, Harvard University, vol. XL, no. 1; Cambridge: The Museum, 1949). See also L. C. Wyman, "Navaho Diagnosticians," *American Anthropologist*, n.s. XXXVIII (1938), 236–246.

[10] In 1949 there were 115 families living in Unit 1, 34 in Unit 2, and 42 in Unit 3.

[11] These two and a delegate from the Burnhams-Bisti areas were chosen as representatives from District 13.

relations of Navahos including marriage, divorce, and inheritance; and administers justice. The Council also expresses opinions regarding government acts and advises the government." [12] Meetings were held two or three times a year or whenever issues warranted. The leading delegate from Fruitland was also a member of a nine-man Tribal Advisory Committee, elected by the Council from its own membership to expedite its large volume of business.

Chapter officers were chosen to deal with local rather than tribal affairs. Their election, also for four-year terms, was not as formal as that of council delegates. Candidates for office, one from each unit, either spoke for themselves or were nominated by someone else. Since there was usually only one nominated for each office, a show of hands constituted election. The elected officers' functions appeared to be three: to announce community meetings, to serve as intermediaries between community members and the local office of the Agency, and to voice their opinions at meetings.

During the spring and summer of 1949 four community meetings were held. At the first, members discussed ditch cleaning and collection of funds to send one delegate with the Advisory Committee to Washington. [13] The second concerned new land assignments and the results of the delegates' trip to Washington; the third, a proposed revision of stock regulations and the sheep-dipping date; and the fourth, grasshopper control. At all these meetings six or seven Navahos consistently dominated discussion. All of them had been chapter officers in the past except

[12] Kluckhohn and Leighton, *The Navaho*, p. 102.

[13] A trader from across the river advanced more than $100 for the delegate's expenses. At each of the succeeding meetings the chapter officer from Unit 1 urged the people to donate funds in order that the debt could be repaid. One young Navaho commented, "Only the poor people contribute money. The rich people don't help out, but they sure talk at meetings."

a former policeman, who had been discharged by the supervisor because he "talked against the government."

One council delegate, a community leader for many years, received his primary support from the closely knit community in Unit 2. Earlier he had championed the cause against stock reduction. Now, though he agreed with the government on issues which he felt would help the community, he either carefully avoided discussing or else opposed government proposals which were emotionally charged. He was known to Fruitlanders as one who did not fear the government and who always consulted them on issues before appearing at council meetings or discussing community problems with the Agency at Window Rock.[14]

The second delegate played a minor role at meetings in the summer of 1949, perhaps because he was employed by the Agency but primarily because he was not a recognized resident of the community. He and his wife had moved into Unit 1 from Burnhams years before but had not built a permanent home. A mild man, he was influenced by a strong-willed sister who believed that councilmen were government-controlled and who did not wish to see her brother in that role. He lacked influence in the community and confined his activities to interceding in the numerous domestic quarrels, for example, by sheltering women threatened by their husbands. (In contrast, the leading delegate would have nothing to do with personal problems; when confronted by families demanding compensation from boys who supposedly had seduced their daughters, he merely laughed off the incident.)

In the late 1940's there were three chapter officers, one from

[14] If this reputation was not quite accurate, it was sufficiently widespread to gain him wide backing. As Kluckhohn and Leighton indicate in *The Navaho*, p. 178, fear of accusations of witchcraft restrains leaders from assuming too much power. See also *ibid.*, p. 69.

each of the units. The chapter officer from Unit 1 was a man well over seventy. He had moved into Fruitland long before the new canal was built, and the people felt that he was one of the better farmers. At meetings he frequently injected "old-fashioned beliefs." During a meeting on livestock matters, he urged the stockmen to abandon the practice of dipping sheep because he said the fumes from the dips caused people to contract tuberculosis.

The elderly man who had represented Unit 3 died in late 1949 and was replaced by a singer. The singer was an agreeable man, much respected by the Unit 3 residents and well known for his skill until he became afflicted with throat spasms, which people said resulted from "un-Navaho" behavior at a ceremony.

The chapter president, from Unit 2, belonged to one of the largest outfits (a group of relatives larger than the extended family who regularly co-operated for certain purposes) in Fruitland. His family group included about fifty members, of whom eight held farm assignments. He was supposed to inform the people in his unit of meetings, to attend sessions of the Land Assignment Committee, and to preside over general community meetings. But he spent most of the summer of 1950 with one and then another singer in the hope of curing his ailing daughter. On one occasion he spent three weeks at Carson with the female shaman. She told him who was "witching" his daughter.[15]

[15] The Carson woman was said to have been responsible for "pointing" her finger toward at least two other supposed "witches." Almost inevitably, she was herself accused, more than once: "That woman is a witch, and she lost some business. They used to take money, jewelry, blankets, and everything to the woman, but now people don't take her much even when they go to see her. They found that she is a bad woman, causing sickness in some people, and telling people that different Indians were witching somebody. . . . They say that that woman is the leader of the 'Navaho Wolves.' The 'Navaho Wolves' get their power and speed when that woman sings and beats the drum in her hogan. When she stops, the wolves stop and rest. When she starts again, the wolves begin to run. The wolves go around to different hogans and see what is going on. Then

The president's sons, both veterans of the war in Europe, embarrassed him by brawling. He felt the force of ostracism resulting from this aberrant behavior. He could no longer introduce his speeches at community meetings with the traditional disclaimer, "I can say what I want to because I have done no wrong."

From the start of the government Irrigation Project, federal employees were aware of differences in the social patterns of the three units.[16] One employee, no longer with the Agency, remarked that mostly "agitators" lived in Unit 2, "co-operators" in Unit 1, and "neutrals" in Unit 3. He classified the veterans as "unco-operative and shiftless" in Unit 2, "co-operative and progressive" in Unit 1, and "co-operative but shiftless" in Unit 3. His remarks, although indicative of traditional prejudice against Navahos, had a basis in fact. The political behavior of each of the three units did indeed differ, for it reflected social organization, with Unit 2 conforming closest to ancient Navaho tradition. There the organization existing before construction of the canal was least disturbed, since all irrigable land had long since been occupied. With few new residents and with all but two

---

they put sickness into that hogan. When they do that, they go back to that woman. Then the man who has a sick person in the family comes to her and asks her to sing with the feathers. She tells them who is witching the sick person, and leaves it up to the man to find the right medicine man. But the young people don't believe that medicine man can cure that sickness. They go right out and take some kind of action."

[16] Besides the distinction between the three units as geographical and social entities, Fruitland Navahos differentiated themselves into original settlers, including men who had married into local families before the construction of the old Jensen and Curley ditches in the 1920's; farmers who received land at the time of the Jensen and Curley ditches; and farmers who came to the Project with the new canal system. They subdivided the last group into those who came in from outside District 13 as transient laborers to work with the Civilian Conservation Corps during the middle 1930's and those who came from the Burnhams-Bisti areas within District 13 after the completion of the new canal.

families comprising parts of larger extended families which in turn were linked with two outfits, the long-time co-operating social units functioned much like the traditional Navaho society described by Kimball and Provinse:

Navaho society is no simple grouping of individuals in distinct and separate families, with each family unit comprising the totality of persons who, working together, satisfy all the needs or wants of the social group. The family is an important institution which orders and directs much of the behavior and activity of its members, but simple observation reveals that there are many instances in which necessary activities are performed by persons drawn from several families. Further observation reveals that some operations, such as plowing or planting, bring together persons who also do many other things together, and that in these cooperative efforts there is direction and leadership which appears on all occasions that demand the combined efforts of a cooperative unit larger than the family.[17]

Instead of strengthening the economic position of Unit 2, the new enlarged canal weakened it, for initially the government required that stockmen reduce their sheep before acquiring an assignment. The people of Unit 2 also objected to the disruption of their previous political organization. From the beginning they mustered their forces to attack government agents and policies. The delegate and the chapter officer, outspoken men themselves, could always rally sufficient support from their relatives to overrule suggestions for change even when they were agreed to by the other units. Considerable social and psychological pressures were brought to bear on persons who might wish to co-operate with the government.

The elders of Unit 2 were concerned, even before the opening of the new canal, lest their children move away from the reservation or discard old Navaho ways; they managed to hold their young men by marrying them to local non-English-speak-

[17] Solon T. Kimball and John Provinse, "Navajo Social Organization in Land Use Planning," *Applied Anthropology*, I (1942), 20.

ing Navaho girls. Once married to such a girl, a man had to stay with his wife's parents if he were a good Navaho son-in-law, or he had to leave the reservation. Men from Sanostee, Red Rock, Shiprock, and Lukachukai and from other areas also married local girls and lived with their wives' families.

At the same time, young Fruitlanders brought in wives from other areas; the newly married couples were given the use of small plots of farmland. When the government took over the canal system in 1936 and required the keeping of records, farmers in Unit 2 simply formalized land-use agreements already in existence. During the excavation of the big canal few outsiders married local girls, and only two outsiders obtained farms in Unit 2. As more land became available, sons of the original settlers in Unit 2 obtained land assignments, and extended families quite legally held not ten but fifty or more acres.

In this unit, unlike the others, few families resided at sheep camps in winter. These were but a few miles south and could be reached easily. However, in Unit 2, as elsewhere, family life was often disrupted during the winter by off-reservation employment and by the attendance of children at boarding schools. But in summer husband, wife, and unmarried children were consistently together and were integrated members of their extended family, working and visiting together frequently. In many cases, they saw nothing of neighbors outside their own extended families except for business transactions or when asked to help at ceremonials. The in-group feelings of long-time residents in a rather restricted geographical area, who had maintained strong family and outfit relationships, gave their whole community great social cohesion. In 1948, when the local supervisor attempted to enforce the livestock-permit ruling on a widow who owned horses, her relatives (including clan relatives) rose in a body to protest, insisted that she be permitted to keep her "extra" horses, and called for a general reinvestigation of the farmers' needs. Perhaps because of their resistance, the farmers of Unit 2 possessed a disproportionate share of livestock on the Project. Though representing less than 20 per cent of the population, they owned more than half the animals.

Leadership in Unit 2 was in the hands of three non-English-speaking Navahos, all related by marriage. Young English-speaking men participated only informally in community politics, attending community meetings but playing no active role. (At home, during meal times or when they made informal visits to their relatives' homes, they had the prerogative of discussing community problems "because," as one Navaho pointed out, "they are related.") Fathers told sons with land assignments of their own what should be planted and what actions they should take with respect to their own problems or those of the unit or the Project as a whole. Men married to local girls were subservient to their fathers-in-law. Even fathers who were no longer physically active sometimes continued to function in an advisory capacity.

The younger men, especially those who married into the community, found themselves obligated to help their relatives; but their in-laws reciprocated. Younger men plowed and irrigated, lent hay, and performed many heavy tasks. In return, their elders bailed them out of jail, cared for their wives and children when they went away to work, and contributed to the expenses of curing rites. In all these particulars, Unit 2 came nearest of the three units in Fruitland to approximating the traditional pattern of Navaho culture.

Although it is by far the largest of the three, Unit 1, which is physically closest to Farmington, has never had the cohesiveness, and consequently the social power, of Unit 2. Originally settled (like Unit 2) by members of several extended families, Unit 1, easily absorbed its first influx of outsiders during the 1920's. Most of these "outsiders" were given ten acres of land in exchange for labor on the Jensen ditch system. Many were actually related to the old resident farmers either by blood or by marriage. They were "outsiders" in name only. When the new canal was completed in 1938, sufficient land became available both for the sons of resident farmers and for newcomers, who soon comprised 60 per cent of the population. A considerable number of the original landholders living near the river's edge moved to new assignments closer to the main canal and sometimes to Unit 3, where larger assignments were available. An additional motive to leave Unit 1 was concern over the increasing amount of alkali on old fields, which was attributed to seepage of water from the main canal. Thus, overwhelmed by a rush of outsiders and deserted by its own leadership, the old society disintegrated.

Naturally, the "first families" of Unit 1 and the early settlers of the 1920's (who had slowly been converted into "older inhabitants") objected to the stock-reduction program and land-assignment system which were inaugurated in the late thirties. Like the stockman of Unit 2, they did not wish to lose their animals. But this limited basis for agreement never gave them the cohesion of Unit 2, for many Unit 1 "inhabitants" who owned livestock kept them at sheep camps as far as thirty miles to the south. They maintained their permanent homes at Burnhams or Bisti or elsewhere and lived in tents and brush shelters when on the Project. Many of these men visited their farms only when work needed to be done and were not so intimately tied to the Project as the people of Unit 2.

In addition, there were very real social differences among the farmers of Unit 1, quite apart from their areas of origin. Many young men of Unit 1, trained in off-reservation schools, spoke English and commanded technical knowledge that enabled them to obtain positions with the government. More individualistic than the few men of their own age group who had married into families in Unit 2, they did not participate in community meetings. Without extended-family ties in the immediate vicinity, they were, within limits, able to behave as they pleased. Like the rest of the Project's most "progressive" farmers—that is, those willing to work with and even for the Agency—they tended to keep themselves in physical as well as social isolation.

Finally, Unit 1 differed from Unit 2 in that the resentments occasioned by stock reduction did not last long and were not so vigorously cherished. As one Navaho in Unit 1 declared, "If a fellow has fifteen acres, two horses is all he can get on with. I have two horses and that is enough [for sixteen acres]. . . . Some of those fellows [in Unit 2] still have the old idea that lots of horses give prestige and power, that kinda stuff." Such a response was practical, rational, individual—neither emotionally nor traditionally based.

Within Unit 1 was a small group of older English-speaking Navahos. These men were mostly graduates of Carlisle Indian Institute in Pennsylvania, Haskell Institute in Kansas, Fort Lewis in Colorado, mission schools in the vicinity, or the Navaho Service boarding schools at Shiprock and Fort Wingate, New Mexico. They had returned from rigid, military education resentful over their treatment at the hands of school officials and had then been made to feel by "long-hairs" (traditionally oriented Navahos) that they were the "maladjusted" minority in Navaho society. As a result, this group differed in outlook from those younger English speakers whose experiences of white culture were perhaps more satisfying. Most had worked at one time for the government, and most had served a term as community leaders, but they now seemed little interested in public affairs. A former chapter officer reflected the group's attitude: "I don't know anything about politics. I just keep clear. It's too much headache. Those delegates are just like scarecrows. Whatever they say doesn't mean a damned thing to the government."

Thus neither the young "progressives" nor the older men who had been to "white" schools were active in community politics. Their failure may have been due to their past or present government jobs. The most capable and most mature planners were considered "pets" of the government, and hence distrusted. Perhaps to some extent they were "Agency Indians . . . encouraged by whites to feel superior to the rest of the Indian community, including their own relatives . . . , cut off from contemporary Navaho society and subjected to resentment and ridicule by their fellow tribesmen, yet not accepted as full equals by Reservation White society." [18] In the earlier days of the Project some had attempted to form a farm association, but after repeated failures they became discouraged. These were the farmers who owned tractors and did custom plowing and cultivating or owned various other types of mechanical equipment. During the war the educated men of Unit 1 who were not in the armed forces saw more of non-Navahos than did members of Unit 2; they learned many farming and animal-husbandry practices. Although they helped at squaw dances and at curing rites when requested, they sought the less expensive curing methods offered by the mission hospital and by private clinics in town. Hence not only was Unit 1 socially less cohesive than Unit 2 and organized along less rigid lines, but it also included a larger proportion of men favorably oriented to the white culture or at least not actively hostile to it.

Unit 3 was the least organized of all. Many farms did not have houses or hogans. Tents were used during the busy season, but they were taken down when their occupants left for home elsewhere. The farms were larger here, and the people lived farther apart. Although there was an elected chapter officer, most problems were handled by local kin groups consulting with government agents or by individuals and agents. There was little concerted action by residents of the group for government services or co-operation with the other units. For example, although Unit 3 farms frequently suffered from water shortages, as they occupied a position at the end of the canal, farmers did not as a body request rationing; they either made their protests in-

[18] Kluckhohn and Leighton, *The Navaho*, p. 106.

dividually or left their farms. There was little antigovernment sentiment, for the people had moved in after the assignment-size question was settled. Most had received twenty acres; and whereas preference was given to veterans without livestock, ownership of animals did not prevent sheepmen from acquiring land.

Unit 3 was opened for cultivation several years after the others. A few farms had existed early in the century, but they were washed away in the flood of 1911. The new canal made fifty-seven farms available between 1940 and 1948. Not only was the soil considered by the Navahos to be better than that in Unit 1 or 2, but the land was available in larger assignments. Some of those who settled were relatives of farmers in Unit 1, but over 60 per cent came from the plateau to the south of the Project and from Burnhams and Bisti.

Fifty per cent of the farmers in Unit 3 owned sheep in 1950, as opposed to 35 per cent in Unit 1. As land became available during and especially after the war, the government issued farms first to returning students and veterans. Generally these men did not own sheep; but other later applicants who did were no longer questioned closely about livestock holdings. As a result, the farmers here were generally unconcerned or "neutral" about federal livestock policies.

Because of its newness, almost all land was in alfalfa during the 1940's. Consequently Navahos on Unit 3 could absent themselves from their farms a great deal of the time. There were still fewer permanent structures than in Unit 1 and less social interaction. During the harvest season a few neighbors worked together, and individual farmers called on their relatives, but most residents of Unit 3 hired what labor they needed.

There were very few extended-family groups in Unit 3; though kinship lines linked some with families in Units 1 and 2, residents of these other units seldom visited in Unit 3. People in Unit 3 visited more frequently, passing through the other units on their way to town. Visits were lengthy only during curing rites.

Characterized by government employees as "neutral," only a few Unit 3 residents participated in Project meetings. They did not consider Fruitland their home but oriented their social life around the community of their origin. They conducted little business with each other or with government agents, perhaps because on farm matters they had no reason to quarrel with the government. They were often absent when agents visited their farms.

CHAPTER V

Washington and District 13

PAST misunderstandings between Indians and Indian Service are part of Fruitland history and a major cause of present frustration. Such misunderstandings as still existed in 1950 were both a misfortune to be explained in terms of the past and an influence bearing upon the future. Some government employees continued to show contempt for and ignorance of Navaho ways; their contempt was naturally matched by Fruitland mistrust of the government.

The same ideas about Navahos as characterized the people of Farmington led some Indian Service workers to attempt paternalistic management of a people considered childlike and led others to forget that Navahos are human. For example, an Indian Service official on field trips often took along an interpreter whom he chose to perceive as somehow non-Indian and in whose presence he spoke thoughtlessly and disparagingly about Indians in general. Embarrassment, hostility, and a lowering of the Navaho employee's self-esteem and job satisfaction naturally resulted. (On the other hand, non-Navaho government employees sometimes developed a feeling of being "inferior" because they worked with what they believed "inferior" people.)

Indian agents often overlooked Navaho cultural patterns in implementing programs. For example, women traditionally have high status in Navaho society and often achieve economic importance through their skill and devotion in the care of sheep and goats, but negotiations regarding credit and land assignment were invariably carried out with men. Although non-English-speaking Navahos comprised about 70 per cent of the assignees, agency personnel tended to spend more time with those who spoke English and to give them most of the available jobs. One farmer complained that those in Unit 1 were the ones who got the government jobs. The preferential treatment given to younger men acted as an irritant in a society where elders traditionally have prerogatives. The generalized categories employed by a government employee, "co-operative" or "shiftless," resulted in such comments as, "That man doesn't like The People, and The People don't like him."

Fruitlanders classified agency people as "for" or "against" the Navahos, depending upon how flexible they were in carrying out their duties. There was a general feeling that "Washindoon" left only the incompetent in Fruitland. Whenever any differences arose, Fruitlanders often confused issues with personalities. Salary as well as cultural differences between Navaho and non-Navaho school employees sometimes led to an indiscriminate condemnation of policy. Older Indians condemned the schools for insisting that children speak English but at the same time praised mission schools for producing pupils who had learned to speak English well at the sacrifice of knowledge of their own culture. "Washindoon" and Window Rock were symbols of confusion and dissatisfaction; they were associated with frequent changes in policy and rapid change-over in personnel.[1]

The important links between Washington, or "policy," and

[1] Traders often seemed to enjoy rather than sympathize with the difficulties encountered by the government personnel. Government hiring through civil service channels (which implies the bringing in of employees

the Fruitland Navahos were the Indian Service employees who have face-to-face contacts with the Fruitlanders. Upon this relationship depended much of the success of programs designed to aid the Indians. In broad terms, the duty of employees was not to work for the Indians but to teach them to work for themselves and to give them encouragement and leadership. These positions called for men and women with understanding of differences between their own culture and that of the Indians; with courage and perseverance to cope with slow progress, limited working budgets, and difficulties in living conditions; with imagination and flexibility in adjusting Indian Service programs to fit into the social and psychological state of the community in which they worked. The importance of the supervisor, the technically trained extension worker and irrigation engineer, and the teachers and other professionals connected with the Indian Service cannot be overemphasized in assessing the situation at Fruitland. When Fruitlanders discovered that a government worker sympathized with their problems and could handle relationships well, they considered him as "for the Navahos." Another employee just as sympathetic but unable to think in "Navaho" terms was considered to be "against" them.

----

from a distance) limited the acceptance of government agents by local people on any social level. A strong in-group feeling has developed among the local non-Navahos over a period of years. The Agency in turn utilized the traders only as a means of communicating notice of coming events to the Navahos. The complete lack of shared discussion of basic problems and of methods for solving them tended to increase the traders' latent resentment—and their amusement when programs failed. James West, in *Plainville, U.S.A.* (New York: Columbia University Press, 1947), p. 218, describes resistances to modern technology by a rural folk in an isolated area: "Perhaps more would 'believe,' and believe sooner, if sociological techniques were devised to disseminate the new knowledge through local leadership other than that of a few relatively 'rational' farmers. . . . The county agent, aside from ignoring the lower class and its leaders, makes little or no effort to win the influence of merchants, lodge members, or ordinary school teachers."

Whether the turnover in personnel during the 1930's and early 1940's came as a result of the tense situation existing at Fruitland or whether it came as a result of the depression and the war was to the Navahos quite beside the point. The Navahos knew only that some men whom they considered "for the Navahos" were transferred after short periods in residence. Thus, in 1943 when the local extension agent suggested that the farmers purchase a wheat combine, the local chapter officer urged that it be bought without delay before the agent could be transferred or inducted into the army.[2] Farmers also took more interest in vegetable gardening as a result of that agent's stimulation; he planted, distributed plants, and instructed the farmers. But shortly he left. The wheat combine was not bought; acreage in gardens diminished. By contrast, an agent who had proved himself a capable technician but was considered "against the Navahos" remained with the Project for over five years.

Agency personnel at the local level must contend with many difficulties beyond their control. Their monetary compensation, recognition, and other satisfactions are meager; their positive accomplishments are often taken for granted by the Navahos. But not the least of their difficulties is what seems to the Navahos to be a policy of arbitrary transfers.

The formal administrative head of the Fruitland Project was the supervisor, assigned to carry out on the community level the complete services rendered in non-Navaho communities by local, county, state, and federal agencies in the fields of general administration, natural resources, engineering, and community services. Under his general direction the irrigation engineer, the farm-management supervisor, the school principal, and such visiting officials as public health nurses, sanitary engineers, and welfare workers performed the services required to promote the smooth functioning of the community. Each branch was also directed by specialized technicians in the central Navajo

[2] Minutes of Community Meeting, Aug. 5, 1943.

Agency at Window Rock.[3] These multiple official lines of authority and communication, as will be brought out, did not always make for efficient operation of the local agency.

The supervisor's position was difficult. He had to follow federal rules and regulations but constantly be aware of the effects on the Navahos of strict, impersonal adherence to rules. Many general directives did not apply to his particular area of responsibility; indeed, their application was usually determined by his interpretation.[4]

One supervisor, whose primary interest was in livestock and who had successfully reduced livestock in another Navaho area to the carrying capacity of the range, undertook a similar reduction at Fruitland. Since sheep had been reduced to the number permitted, he concentrated on range and farm-horse permits.[5] Range horses were permitted to feed off the browse and grass of nonfarm areas; farmers without grazing permits

[3] In 1950 Indian Service personnel with closest relationships to the Fruitland Navahos were organized as shown in Appendix C.

[4] Kluckhohn and Leighton, in *The Navaho*, p. 109, remark of supervisors generally: "Many are highly conventional, prejudiced, and of limited imagination and flexibility . . . ; it is small wonder that policies which, as conceived in Washington or at Window Rock, take into consideration the ways and needs of the Navaho, are sometimes translated into action which is at the opposite pole from the original intent. Occasionally this is due to intentional sabotage, which is a way of expressing pent-up resentment of low pay, inadequate recognition, and generally unsatisfying living conditions. Again, policies formulated at the top are unconsciously negated and reversed because they have been inadequately explained to field personnel [or] run counter to the employees' lifelong habits and attitudes."

[5] R. K. Merton, in his "Bureaucratic Structures and Personality," *Social Forces*, XVIII (1940), 564, notes: "The official is tacitly expected to and largely does adapt his thoughts, feelings and actions to the prospects of his career. But these very devices which increase the probability of his conformance also lead to an overconcern with strict adherence to regulations which induce timidity, conservatism, and technicism. Displacement of sentiments from goals onto means is fostered by the tremendous significance of the means (rules)."

could keep farm horses on condition that they were fed the products of the farms and kept within the fenced area of individual assignments. Stray animals were to be impounded in the government corral and charges assessed for damages and for feed during impoundment.

The supervisor was fulfilling his nominal duty when he impounded stray horses. But some Navahos, particularly those who still felt hostile because of the stock-reduction program, threatened and abused him. The supervisor was seriously concerned:

He was insulting me in front of the Superintendent, and I wasn't going to take it. I walked out. When he [the delegate, M. C.] asked me why I wasn't going to take any of that running-down, I told M. C. that I was willing to come to any of the meetings to explain directives and policies, and try to help the Navahos out, but as for taking insults, nothing doing.

His reaction to the abuses resulted in further mutual intolerance. His relationship with the progressive English-speaking Navahos, however, remained fairly good. He tended to spend more time with the people whom he considered co-operative, and he gave available work to the members of this group.

Unavoidable delays, "red tape," and policy changes beyond the control of the supervisor have been sources of tension, for Indians had little understanding of Indian Bureau operations. Any delay in payment of money, especially, brought about accusation of double-dealing or stealing. Such accusations were directed at the supervisor when he did not immediately issue checks following the sale of over-age horses at Gallup. The Navahos apparently were not told beforehand that buyers had to be found and that all such transactions took time. The supervisor's response to the situation was to call the Indians troublemakers who had little appreciation of the services that he gave them.

The supervisor worked more than the forty-hour week required of federal employees. For overtime he received neither extra pay nor other rewards from the Indian Service. Lack of recognition for extra duty has caused many field employees to avoid overtime—but it was on the basis of extra work that Indian Service personnel was judged by Navahos.

During the spring of 1949 a new supervisor was placed in charge. Like his predecessor, this man had a successful record of twelve years in the Navajo Service. But, unlike his predecessor, he carefully avoided those areas which he considered particularly sensitive. Instead of assuming the responsibility for carrying out directives from Window Rock, he worked closely with the Navahos. In other words, he operated on the basis of a "let-alone" policy until such a time as the Navahos solved the questions which bothered them. He felt that if the Navahos had problems they would come to him for help. Furthermore, he was patient and listened to the people and rarely said anything at community meetings. One Navaho, comparing him with the former supervisor, said that this man listened whereas the former supervisor did all the talking. When a rumor was circulated in the community that the new supervisor was going to be forced to resign, one "agitator" (the previous supervisor's classification) remarked, "I guess he is too easy on the Navahos."

The irrigation engineer was in charge of the technical aspects of the water system. Under his supervision were three Navaho technicians who subjugated land and helped maintain the irrigation system with draglines, tractors, and other machinery. His duties were technical, but occasionally he was called upon to sit with the supervisor, the tribal delegates, and chapter officers in making land-assignment decisions. In the organizational hierarchy of the Project, he was subordinate to the supervisor, but he maintained direct channels of communication with the chief of the Irrigation Division at Window Rock. Thus, he served two masters. He served as second in command in the absence of the supervisor.

Although the irrigation engineer did not have direct contact with the community at large, the men under his supervision were, significantly, the most progressive farmers in the Project. Two of the employees owned, and hired laborers to operate, tractors, a hay baler, and a bean thresher. Their time was divided between government work and their farms, and incomes from the two sources gave them a more stable home and economic life than was possible for farmers who worked part time away from the reservation.

The school operated as an independent division with its lines of communication going through the Shiprock Agency and thence to Window Rock. But people and supervisor alike considered the school as part of over-all local services. As a supervisor said in 1941 at a community meeting,

they are planning on having a high school here. They can take care of seventy day school children and fifty high school children. If we are going to cut the sheep units down to suit the range, then we should get more education so that our children will have better jobs. It is a good subject to bring up and I want to tell you that it is through the efforts of you Delegates and Chapter Officers that you will get a better school.[6]

The Fruitlanders had believed that the focus of the school would be on agricultural subjects, but slashing of appropriations, shortages in personnel, and the war blasted their hopes.[7]

[6] Minutes of Community Meeting, April 21, 1941.

[7] John Collier, the former Commissioner of Indian Affairs, writes of the difficulties which the Navajo Service faced in implementing such programs, in his "United States Indian Administration as a Laboratory of Ethnic Relations," *Social Research*, XII (1945), 293–294: "The 'Technical Cooperation,' Bureau of Indian Affairs . . . was directed by the Indian Service but financed from temporary funds of the Department of Agriculture. It put into the field groups of specialists who, working together, studied and planned in rather swift succession on a large number of Indian Reservations. The group included soils and water specialists, agronomists, anthropologists, and specialists in social economy. The work was very competent indeed, and was integrative of the relevant specialities,

Shortly after the war the day school was converted to a semi-boarding-type school (to which the children were brought early Monday morning and from which they returned to their homes Friday evening). With the closing of the day school at Burnhams during the war, the children from all over District 13 were recruited for the Fruitland School.

A principal was in charge of the school, with administrative help from a head teacher. In 1949 these two, with a staff of three teachers, composed the non-Navaho members of the institution. The Navaho staff included a cook, a boys' adviser, a matron, a farmer, a fireman, and several men hired as irregular laborers. Except when in the classroom, the children were under the care of the matron and the boys' adviser; under the supervision of these two, they helped clean dormitories, classrooms, and playground. Some of the older boys on occasion helped unload supplies. The non-Navaho staff members, except for two teachers who lived across the river, were quartered in the better apartments, which were furnished with fairly adequate furniture. The Navaho employees lived in buildings far inferior and with inadequate furnishings. Their rentals, in keeping with the salary scale, were much lower. Nevertheless the difference in quality

---

but because of the fund limitations it had to be conducted on a fast schedule. Therefore, it could not wait until a felt need, related to action, had been evoked from employed personnel or from Indians in the jurisdictions. . . . It could not veer its data and recommendations back into action programs. And more subtly and factually, the staff itself was prevented by the severe time factor from reaching down into the highly particular context of stresses and strains, informal as well as formal social organizations, traditions, limitations, and all the other factors which in their totality were the resistant and dynamic whole of the human-environmental communities that were being studied. Some hundreds of thousands of dollars were spent in this enterprise of research. . . . What they were striving for was action-research, research action, and participation by administrators and local laity. But their budget demanded quantity production, and it had to be spent in a limited time. Their operative and practical aims alike were marred as soon as born."

of quarters was of concern to some and was no doubt reflected in their attitudes.

There was little "socializing" between the non-Indian and Navaho employees, perhaps partly because they were in close association with each other all day but more likely because they had no mutual interests. Moreover, the Navaho employees of the school did not associate with other Navaho government employees or with other Navahos in the community. The farmer and his wife (the cook) spent their weekends at their home near Chaco Canyon; the matron spent her free time in Gallup or with her family in Farmington; the regular fireman returned to his home at Shiprock. The boys' adviser alone maintained continuous relationships with The People in the community. In his free time he visited clan relatives.

Of significance in the relationship between school and community was the attitude expressed by several of the Navaho employees toward native cultural beliefs. They considered themselves "educated" and above practicing native curing rites; they spoke disparagingly about the nonliterate Navahos. Only one Navaho employee, in spite of his five years in the armed services, still overtly adhered to many of the traditional ways and beliefs.

The Navahos compared this local government school with the Methodist mission school in Farmington, an institution in existence for over fifty years. The mission school, they knew, was accredited by the state of New Mexico, and several of its Fruitland graduates had entered college. More important, its alumni seemed to have greater facility in the use of the English language.[8] But whereas the government school was obligated to take all children, the mission school was highly selective and chose its students from applicants all over the Navaho and Hopi reservations. In particular, the mission school took chil-

[8] See Tom T. Sasaki and David L. Olmsted, "Navaho Acculturation and English-Language Skills," *American Anthropologist*, n.s. LV (1953), 80–99.

dren from families already possessing some education and already acculturated. Whereas the government school could only attempt to enforce regular attendance, the mission school could dismiss irregular students and replace them from a waiting list. Whereas the government school did not enforce the use of the English language, the mission school, again with the same leverage, required it. And whereas the government school, though co-operating with missionaries, did not request students to give up their religion, the mission school did.

One last contrast appeared to affect markedly the Navahos' judgment about the two schools. The mission school required tuition fees, but the government institution was open to children without cost; and the value placed on the "cost" of services or goods has long played an important part in determining the Navahos' attitudes toward services. Fees are paid to singers, to "diagnosticians," or to silversmiths when services are received.[9] When he pays, the Navaho believes that he can expect to get better services and goods. Furthermore, no Navaho likes to be ridiculed about having been bettered in a bargain and will express satisfaction with the services or goods received whether or not they are truly high quality.[10]

[9] Cf. John Adair, *The Navajo and Pueblo Silversmiths* (Norman: University of Oklahoma Press, 1955), p. 96: "The Navajo buying the bracelet would then take it and he would feel proud because he had paid so much money for it. A smith is doing the Navajo a favor when he sells him jewelry for a high price, because then the buyer can boast of how much he paid."

[10] Alexander H. and Dorothea C. Leighton, in *The Navaho Door* (Cambridge: Harvard University Press, 1944), p. 36, say in reference to curing rites: "The Navahos like ourselves develop strong faith in anything that has cost them time, money, and thought and are reluctant to have it said that the ceremonial was after all a failure."

CHAPTER VI

Interlude: Analysis of Fruitland in 1950

IN this chapter the preceding data will be summarized analytically. For purposes of this analysis the conceptual framework previously used by Leighton [1] and others [2] in dealing with situations of social and psychological tensions will be utilized. The material will be summarized in the light of the concept of dynamic or moving equilibrium, to discover the functional relationships of stress and culture among the Fruitland Navahos.

[1] Alexander H. Leighton's use of the concept of dynamic equilibrium as an analytical tool in the study of society is largely unpublished. However, as applied to an individual, a statement may be found in his and Dorothea C. Leighton's *Gregorio, the Hand Trembler*. The concept is also summarized in the unpublished master's thesis by Frank B. Miller, "Three Approaches to Human Relations" (New York State School of Industrial and Labor Relations, Cornell University, 1948), and in the unpublished doctor's thesis by Manet Fowler, "The Case of Chef A: An Inquiry into and Analysis of a Human Relations Situation" (Cornell University, 1954).

[2] See Kingsley Davis, *Human Society* (New York: Macmillan Company, 1950), pp. 634–635. See also Melvin Tumin, *Caste in a Peasant Society* (Princeton: Princeton University Press, 1952), pp. 6–7.

The concept of dynamic equilibrium in analyzing change is particularly useful since the question of determinism is not raised; rather, the student can perceive how any variable may trigger changes in other variables.[3]

Although considerable strain was imposed upon the social structure from the time of the Navahos' captivity at Fort Sumner, almost a century ago, analysis here will begin with the mid-1930's. It will show that strains began to mount from this time on but that the bearers of the culture had sufficient vitality to prevent too many new types of social behavior from becoming manifest. In spite of strain, the Fruitland Navahos remained oriented toward the Navaho way, in a condition of uneasy equilibrium.

Equilibrium implies a balance of opposed forces, some of which contribute to the insecurity and others to the security of the group. These opposing forces do not act directly against each other, but the group reacts to them in contrary measures on the basis of its own past experiences, its environment (which is dynamic, that is to say, constantly changing in constituents), and its established patterns of behavior and interaction. Changes in these reaction patterns are brought about through biological reproduction, death, and immigration and emigration over a period of time. In the changes themselves patterns can be observed and described.

When change is introduced slowly, the compensations which the group develops are usually adequate to bring about a new state of equilibrium without undue stress to the functional integrity of the whole. However, in the periods of rapid change which are characteristic of modern societies, the adjustive and adaptive [4] mechanisms are overwhelmed and fail to cope with

[3] Davis, *Human Society*, p. 634.

[4] Kluckhohn, in *Navaho Witchcraft*, p. 46, defines "adaptive" and "adjustive" as follows: " 'Adaptive' is a purely descriptive term referring to

change. Maladaptations occur which serve to increase stress rather than to establish an equilibrium in which stress is kept within tolerable limits. Maladaptation comes about when no social organization or belief system exists capable of coping with rapid and radical changes; under these circumstances, the group tends to fall back on patterns of responses which proved satisfactory for other situations even though they were wholly dissimilar. Without an adequate repertoire of compensatory mechanisms, the group tends to try one and then another response, thereby reacting to change in a variety of ways. In a situation where help is given by a "foreign power" or agency to a group undergoing this sort of stress, reactions to change may include a series of random responses—anger and aggression against the agent of change, apathy, or escape.

The concept of "interdependence" is important to this analytic scheme. "Interdependence" means that each part of the cultural structure is functionally or dysfunctionally related to the whole.[5] In less homogeneous cultures or societies the immediate and direct effects of any given element may not be so widespread as secondary effects. In other words, there is a time lag, particularly in underdeveloped countries which have come in contact with the rapidly changing world. To take a hypothetical case: suppose that a segment of a society, perhaps the young, have through education and contact with foreign ideas and technology oriented themselves to norms existing outside their own society. These norms tend to remain latent because the culture of the young people's society is still strong enough

---

the fact that certain types of behavior result in survival. . . . 'Adjustive' refers to those responses which bring about an adjustment of the individual, which remove the motivation stimulating the individual."

[5] For a discussion of the concepts of function and dysfunction see Robert K. Merton, *Social Theory and Social Structure* (Glencoe, Ill.: Free Press, 1949), ch. i.

to prevent wide divergence from its patterns and because the situation itself does not permit free expression of these norms. Major changes may then occur when circumstances permit the manifestation of latent behavior through either weakening of the culture or changes in the situation.

The pages which follow will summarize through the use of equilibrium analysis (1) the adaptations of the Fruitlanders to their environment during the stock-reduction period of the mid-1930's, (2) the condition of equilibrium during the early unsettled years of the Fruitland Project, and (3) the situation at Fruitland during the postwar era. The particular state of equilibrium or disequilibrium—the forces which at the given period seemed to be impinging upon the residents and the residents' responses to these forces—brings out that the community was not homogeneous and that from the start of the Fruitland Project different groups of Fruitlanders have oriented themselves to social forces in slightly different ways. The picture of the Fruitland Project thus given, through the period to 1950, will serve in the later chapters as one basis for judging how each *group* fared when they shifted from a predominantly rural subsistence economy to a wageworking cash economy.

Before the middle 1930's and the introduction of the large canal system, the Fruitland Navahos lived largely on income from livestock. A few had small farms as adjuncts. Although already in process of rapid acculturation, they managed to retain many of their traditional values and much of their social organization. The major portion of their lives, economic, social, and cultural, was oriented toward the reservation, and their interaction with outsiders was limited. They had worked out an equilibrium between the threats to their aboriginal community and the securities found primarily within its framework. Although changes had been rapid, they were not so drastic as to create intolerable stresses, and the Fruitlanders formulated satisfactory compensatory responses. Each successive change had been adapted to fit the culture structure, but at the same time the structure also had undergone change in order to accommodate the new conditions.

The livestock-reduction program which followed closely the fall in market prices in the early 1930's came upon the Fruitlanders as a blow long to be remembered. The threat was heightened by their sudden awareness that it was no longer possible to satisfy their biological needs with what they could extract from the environment or what they could obtain in cash or credit from the traders through the exchange of goods.

The equilibrium of the Fruitland community for the mid-1930's showed the dominant effects of the government stock-reduction program. Fruitland at this time had a population of about 200, of whom many were resident only part of each year. The stress of stock reduction affected subsistence but also produced strains in their social relations, their health and survival, and their systems of belief. However, factors for security also existed which, viewed through their systems of belief and cultural structure, served to cushion the threats brought about by the reduction program.

Stock reduction created an abrupt change in the Navaho economy and produced strains in the social organization. In this setting the government began its program for the development of irrigation projects, including that at Fruitland, in order to relieve the resulting poverty. In approaching the problem the government, however, neglected to take into consideration the interdependence of a number of factors and caused the community to react with aggression and random behavior instead of co-operation. To the original farmers who had also owned livestock the government requirement that they give up their animals in exchange for land was a threat to the existing social organization as well as to their subsistence. They perceived the government's request as a move to equalize and stabilize the economic level of the people, but also to keep them at a perpetual level of bare subsistence. A long tradition of fruitless conflict with the government and with the white world generally helped to prevent resentments generated by stock reduction and land assignment from flaring into violence or other forms of direct action. Instead, there was a great deal of generalized sulky resentment, which found expression primarily in sanctions applied to the newcomers whom the government had introduced into the situation. Traditional Navaho religious beliefs—witchcraft gossip and demands for ceremonial purification, in particular—provided the old, established group of Fruitlanders with their best weapons against the newcomers. On the other hand, one basic economic circumstance militated strongly against the stability of the older group of Navaho traditionalists and their ability to retain control of the community. Ten-acre land assignments, however adequate they might have been for farmers capable of intensive cultivation and modern methods, did not provide more than bare subsistence; and they provided a great deal less than that for some. Hence all members of the community were driven to supplement their farm income with wagework; and herein lay the most obvious fissure through which the Navaho community could be attacked by forces of social change. For wagework was only to be had by contact with and application to the white world.

The newcomers to Fruitland society quickly proved themselves more adaptable than the traditionalists, not only at using the white man's agricultural techniques but at securing outside jobs to supplement their farm incomes. In terms of traditional Navaho values they were subject to odium on many levels. Not only did they lack horses and sheep; they did not even want them or feel a sense of deprivation at not having them. Their lack of resentment against white culture could be interpreted as lack of proper Navaho "patriotism." Since they had no kin ties in the communities, they did not share excess commodities with needy and sometimes improvident relatives. From the Navaho point of view, this was abominable selfishness and social indifference. Because they did not care or know much about ceremonials, they did not spend so much time in community (that is, individually nonprofitable) activities. This was impiety and witchcraft. On every one of these points, as their economic security improved, they were vulnerable to more determined repressive action by the custodians of official Navaho morality. Hence, while the traditionalists rooted their security in social observances hallowed by time and widespread acceptance and in a determined, suspicious hostility toward white culture, the newcomers rooted their security in economic well-being and a relatively passive attitude toward white technique and white culture generally. Equilibrium was maintained within the society only because the newcomers, accepting tacitly a position of inferiority, undertook to conceal, or maintained in a state of latency, their most flagrant departures from Navaho ways.

If the newcomers are considered best adjusted to the area of economic behavior or subsistence and the traditionalists as firmly entrenched in a system of belief, while social relations constituted an intimate, mingled battleground and meeting ground, an interesting index of relative strength is provided by the behavior of both groups in the matter of health. The general rule was that the traditionalists not only made use of Navaho religious rites and curing rituals themselves but also tended to force the newcomers to take part in these rituals. In fact, both groups patronized white doctors and white-operated hospitals and clinics; both groups used the white man's medicines. But the newcomers took part in Navaho curing rituals only under various forms of duress and would have preferred to do without them. Equally powerful, though nonsocial, forms of pressure led the traditionalists to make use of the white man's medicines, though they would have preferred to dispense with them. But in imposing patterns of social behavior by the use of social sanctions (even in the face of physical circumstances which they were forced tacitly to recognize) the traditionalists clearly showed themselves to be socially dominant.

Thus Fruitland before the war represented an uneasy equilibrium of opposed equilibria; the effect of the war was to relax and dissolve many of these tensions without eliminating them. The young and relatively progressive Navahos who entered the armed services were removed from Fruitland and from the entire reservation situation; war work occupied many others and placed them in circumstances where they were forced to adapt to the white man's values. Finally, the simple passage of time softened once-harsh conflicts. Many of the newcomers who in 1940 were strangers had become, by 1946, respected and familiar residents. Navaho values assign great authority to old age; and, in addition, during the war years almost all Fruitlanders had direct experience with a set of values other than those in which they had grown up. Hence, when the war was over and the veterans returned, many of the conflicts of prewar days had subsided or grown less intense. Many white values were accepted tacitly which in earlier days would have caused protest or scandal; conflicts with the white community and with the Indian Agency became gradually less acute, as the scars and dissent in connection with stock reduction faded. More and more Navahos turned to wagework to augment their farm income; more and more new forms of co-operative purchasing and marketing associations began to take the place of the old extended-family and tribal organizations. As a result of this slow erosion of their position, the traditionalist Navaho leaders devoted particular energy to ceremonies for dispelling the evil effect of white contacts. Superficially, this was the same pattern as had prevailed before the war, with the traditional religious views being pitted against new white ways of behavior which promised economic advantage. But a significant shift was implied in the fact that the "progressive-minded" Navahos were no longer attacked. They were not themselves the objects of witchcraft gossip, as formerly, so much as the presumed victims of white infection. They were not bad, just sick. It was a decisive indication of a deep shift in the power relations within Fruitland, a revelation of the fact that the conservative social powers in Navaho society were too weak, and the progressive powers too strong, for the community to be described any longer as in a state of equilibrium.

In fact, the marked disequilibrium of Fruitland in 1950 indicated that the community was ready for a major shift in orientation. In that same year, by coincidence, a vast nearby field of natural gas was tapped for distribution to the West Coast. The Fruitlanders soon saw that their situation had changed. Off-reservation work and its social context were now brought close to the Irrigation Project, and behavior learned elsewhere, but long latent, became manifest. Construction of a plant and laying of pipelines from gas fields to plant and across some 240 miles of reservation land toward the Arizona-California border provided many openings, and by early 1951 more than eighty Fruitland farmers were employed. A drought had reduced their lamb crop, and their farms promised the usual small returns. High wages attracted even those Fruitlanders most Navaho-oriented.

Had no other job opportunities presented themselves, the Fruitlanders might after a brief period of prosperity reverted to an approximation of their old pattern. But almost at once Farmington became a base for oil and uranium prospectors as well as for gas exploration and development; its population increased from some 3,500 in 1950 to over 12,000 in 1952.[6] Housing and road contractors moved in and hired extensively. The government also provided wage-earning opportunities

[6] Estimates provided by the Farmington Chamber of Commerce, 1953.

through new work projects under a long-range rehabilitation program.[7]

At the same time federal and state welfare agencies undertook to aid the aged, the infirm, the needy, and dependent children among the Indians; the Fruitlanders with land allotments east of the reservation began to receive additional income from oil leases.

The force of change also was becoming apparent to Fruitlanders through a series of noneconomic developments. The Tribal Council began to use the secret ballot in elections, increased delegates' salaries and per diem, and reorganized itself to expedite the rapidly increasing volume of business. The federal law prohibiting sale of alcoholic beverages to Indians was repealed.

The process by which the Fruitlanders shifted their orientation may be represented (and no doubt oversimplified) as follows. Working long hours at new jobs, Fruitlanders neglected community meetings and the like; even in traditionalist Unit 2, men had little time for co-operation. Absence from Navaho communities and especially from neighbors who had acted to restrict change gave freedom to those already tending toward new ways. For the first time since before the stock reduction, Navahos could obtain a cash surplus if they were willing to work. These surpluses enabled them to make down payments on pickup trucks. The trucks further affected social organization at Fruitland. Even in Unit 2, ceremonials were scheduled on weekends so that wageworkers (including the most traditional) could attend. If payments were to be made on cars, they could not afford to lose their jobs through absenteeism. Some Navahos began selling wine at ceremonials. Many participants and spectators drank heavily, even though they believed that

[7] *Planning in Action on the Navajo-Hopi Indian Reservations,* Report no. 2 (Washington: Department of the Interior, March 31, 1952), p. 5.

their behavior was contrary to the basic premise of Navaho religion—that of establishing harmony.

Mobility and ready acquisition of cash changed the Fruitlanders' spending habits. Without fully understanding American patterns of determining credit risk, Navahos inadvertently created a circular response in those with whom they did business. They bought freely in town until they exhausted their ready cash, then bought at trading posts on credit, and instead of paying debts on payday made more purchases in town. As their credit at one trading post was terminated, they went to another and another. Traders condemned the Indians for this practice, but they adapted their services; their posts have been remodeled, more goods are for sale, and lower prices have been established for cash customers.

Prosperity, then, had some dangerous consequences for the Fruitland socioculture; although the Fruitlanders had had some preparation for the transition, it was inadequate. Yet a transformation is occurring on the Project which will eventually result in a new social organization based upon the new orientation. The People do not clearly understand the ways of their neighbors, but they are determinedly sending their children to school and learning what they can themselves. The following chapters will be concerned with the effect after 1950 of rising income first on expenditure patterns, next on over-all social patterns and culture, and finally on the family.

CHAPTER VII

The Flood of New Money

WORKING ordinarily at "irregular" jobs until 1950, the Fruit-landers had tended to appear for work irregularly. Wages had not been attractive; on their off-reservation jobs, they were at the mercy of their employers. When, after 1950, steady work became available in the San Juan Valley, many behavioral patterns stemming from previous off-reservation experiences became manifest at home. Although purchase of automobiles and resultant mobility were the most obvious changes, there was a general widening of the social world. Surplus cash enabled the Navahos to make purchases in stores with more varied stock than that offered in trading posts, and wants were created which could be fulfilled only with cash. Some of their money they spent wisely, and some unwisely. Had the increase in income been limited only to the able-bodied or to those who spoke English, groups oriented toward the Navaho way might have organized to make others conform to traditional behavior. But with the community as a whole participating in new opportunities, marked changes affected expenditure patterns, farm practices, hiring policy, and the granting of concessions which would be of benefit to individuals as well as to the whole tribe.[1]

The right of way which the tribe granted the El Paso Natural Gas Company for its pipeline across the reservation was in the form of a twenty-year lease, with the title retained by the tribe. The company paid the tribe $320 a mile, compared to $35 a mile paid to the state of Arizona for outright purchase of state land. In addition, the company agreed to adhere to erosion-control practices of the Indian Service, to reseed scraped land, and to turn over to the tribe all wells dug during construction and the pumping equipment used on the last well drilled on the reservation. The company further agreed to tap the pipeline every five miles on tribal lands, on request, and to reserve 5,000,000 cubic feet of gas a day for consumption within the reservation. With regard to hiring, the contract stipulated that Navahos should have job preference on the reservation and that they must be paid the same wage as non-Navahos for the same kind of work.

The Fruitlanders benefited directly from the company offer to replace the old footbridge across the San Juan. After consultations with the Tribal Council, the company agreed to build a modern vehicular bridge. A bridge was essential so that trucks and equipment could cross the river to maintain and repair the pipeline. In addition, the company was willing to reimburse individual Navahos for damage done to their property. Farmers whose fields of corn or alfalfa were destroyed by trench diggers would be compensated for the full amount of the anticipated crop, and it was agreed that future damage caused by overhauling procedures would be similarly compensated.[2]

In August, 1950, the company began to move its machinery into a field adjoining the Fruitland trading post, and the Navaho Placement and Employment Division began to recruit laborers.

[1] See proceedings of the Navaho Tribal Council, Window Rock, Ariz., Sept. 11–15, 1950, pp. 121 ff.

[2] *The Pipeliner*, XIII (1950), 7–8.

However, when the hod carriers' union from Albuquerque attempted to unionize the Navahos [3] a few weeks later, employment officials discontinued recruiting activities.

The union organizer made his headquarters at Shiprock, where he could keep in close touch with Navajo Service personnel responsible for hiring and where he could talk with large groups in this most thickly populated area of the northeastern part of the reservation. Except for several trips to Fruitland, where he distributed application cards, he spent most of the first month at Shiprock.

At a squaw dance there, the organizer and his interpreter, an army veteran of six years, were asked to speak. Although the content of his speech was not particularly derogatory to the government or to Tribal Council members, the interpreter apparently distorted and added to the speech, giving the audience the impression that the organizer had described the company as an exploitative monster, the tribal councilmen as ineffectual pawns of the government, and the government as a betrayer of The People. In the general excitement at the squaw dance the crowd concurred, but when individual Navahos returned home, they resented such (apparent) attacks by an outsider. Later a small number of Navahos picketed the government employment office, which was closed at that time.

With the government employment service no longer recruiting labor, the company called upon the Fruitland trader. This man had anticipated that the effects of that year's drought would decrease his and the Navahos' income. Although he had remained neutral in discussions between the union and company, his economic interest coincided with the company's. He was aware that the net earnings of the company's employees would be substantial because of the usually high rate of pay and the long work week.

[3] Gordon F. Streib, "An Attempt to Unionize a Semi-literate Navaho Group," *Human Organization*, XI (1952), 23–31.

The trader's understanding of Navaho "psychology," past Navaho wagework behavior, and plain business sense made him an effective informal recruiter. His phone connection to his second store across the river in Unit 2 gave him the further advantage that when labor was urgently needed he had only to call his manager and ask him to recruit some of his customers. All other recruiters had to cross the river on horseback, walk over the old footbridge, or go by way of Farmington, a round trip of some fifty miles.

The council delegate, a customer of the Fruitland trader, maintained a close consulting relationship with him. It was through their efforts that, as the tempo of work accelerated, over eighty employees, including all able-bodied men from Unit 2—from tradition-minded Unit 2—were employed.[4]

Work began simultaneously at several locations on the reservation. In 1950–1951 a total of 303 Navahos worked for the company,[5] most of them as laborers at a wage scale which began at $1.30 per hour. The top pay, $2.75 per hour, was earned by men who handled dynamite. Wages between these two extremes were received by "jack" or air-hammer operators, half-track drivers, welders' helpers, and the like.

Throughout the second half of August and during September and October, Fruitlanders commuted to work. As the pipeline progressed south and west, away from Fruitland, the men reported earlier at the "pickup" station near the trading post, for the commuting distance had lengthened; many were on the road by four thirty in the morning and sometimes reached home after nine at night. The work-week schedule was sixty hours, with time and a half for overtime.

In mid-August, 1950, while the gas company recruited la-

[4] A Farmington physician examined the applicants to determine their health status.

[5] *Navajo-Hopi Placement Service Year Book* (mimeographed; Window Rock: Navajo Service, 1950–1951).

borers, the Indian Service also began to hire Fruitlanders for construction work. Under the reservation-wide ten-year rehabilitation program,[6] concrete irrigation drops were to be built, the main canal extended by six miles, and 400 additional acres of land subjected to cultivation. During the summer of 1950 more than thirty Fruitlanders, mostly from Unit 1, worked for the Agency at from $1.15 to $1.55 per hour for a forty-hour week. Besides four English-speaking equipment operators, about ten persons worked through the fall and winter.

Unit 2 people, so extensively employed by the company, now had no time to express antagonism against the government. Their attitudes toward the English-speaking "government Indians" of Unit 1 also were modified so that the difference in income level between the two groups was reversed, for gas-line workers received almost twice as much as government employees. Unit 2 Navahos who were unable to obtain gas-line employment because of age or substandard health turned now to the government for jobs on work projects.

By mid-1951 most of the work on the gas line was completed, and it appeared that unemployment would soon be widespread. But although the gas company dismissed a few Navahos, other jobs became available. Discoveries of new gas wells prompted the company to lay feeder lines to a processing plant two miles north of the Project. The plant itself, built to extract such impurities as sulphur from raw natural gas, had to be constructed. Moreover, the heavy influx of oil and gas workers from southeastern New Mexico and Texas to Farmington overtaxed the town's housing and service facilities and created a building boom. Businessmen enlarged their establishments, and competitors and speculators moved in. Between 1951 and 1953 three "tent cities" grew up on the outskirts of town. Employ-

[6] *Planning in Action on the Navajo-Hopi Indian Reservations*, Report no. 3, Jan. 1, 1953.

ment was plentiful; Fruitlanders had little difficulty finding jobs on building and road-construction projects. Although wages were not as high as those paid by the gas company, they were favorable, with the average wage scale about $1.25 per hour and only occasional layoffs caused by material shortages or inclement weather. By this time, too, the Navahos were well acquainted with the location of the State Employment Office, and reservation unemployed went there regularly.

As employment in the vicinity increased, interest in farming decreased, and yields dropped. A few tried to farm on Sundays. But most Navahos employed by the gas company neglected to irrigate their alfalfa, bean, and corn fields or left such duties to other members of their immediate families. Co-operative work was impossible because all but old men, women, and children were absent most of the time. The secondary effects of the wage economy were now manifested. Navahos employed to bale or harvest corn asked wages comparable to those paid by non-Navaho farmers across the river, and net profits from the sale of farm products were further reduced.

Junior Begay, a farmer from Unit 2, with eight acres in corn, called on the women in his sister's family and on his wife's relatives sixty miles away to come to help shell the corn. Of his eighty-eight bags of corn, six bags went to his father for the loan of the sheller and two sacks to an older brother who had lent him a planter; from the cash which the trader paid him for the remaining eighty bags (at $3.25 a bag), Junior paid a total of $140 to his sister's family and to his wife's relatives. His net income for the season from eight acres in hybrid corn was $120.00.

In 1951 wagework interfered with spring plowing. Some farmers hired custom-work operators to plow for them. Some in Unit 2, by enforcing kinship prerogatives, managed to get four to six teams to plow fields on Sundays.

The general lack of interest in individual-farm work was shown most clearly at community ditch-cleaning time. Whereas before 1950 most farmers set aside a week or ten days for cleaning ditches, in the spring of 1951 only one-fourth participated. The $2.40 per day (or $4.40 for a man with a team) credited toward irrigation assessments compared very unfavorably with the going wage scale in industry. Most of the employed paid their assessments in cash. The few men who appeared for work at length agreed to do the others' share at wages comparable to those paid by private industry.

During 1951 and 1952 agency employees expressed concern over the increasing number of idle farms. At one meeting the names of some thirty Navahos who were not adequately farming their assignments were read aloud. Navahos who had neglected their fields for several years were threatened with loss of their assignments. Most said that they had intended to plant but had not been able to leave their jobs or that previous plantings had been unsuccessful because of alkali. As the months passed, most farmers did make an effort to establish crops. But those who planted their fields in corn did not irrigate or cultivate, and the weeds engulfed them. The majority planted alfalfa, which required little care during the remainder of the year except for occasional irrigation. Between 1949 and 1952 Fruitland farmers planted 553.86 acres in new alfalfa, while crops which required constant attention decreased proportionately—improved corn from 348.11 to 154.45 acres, beans from 230.62 to 99.92 acres. On the other hand, Indian corn showed a slight increase, from 421.00 to 481.46 acres.[7]

This shift had advantages other than saving time. Alfalfa plantings produced an average of 2.4 tons of hay per acre for the period 1949–1952. Even at prices as low as $25.00 per ton

[7] These figures and those following were taken from the Navajo Service Extension Reports and from field notes.

the value per acre was greater than the general gross crop value
per acre of $48.00 during the same period. Yields of improved
corn at 28.4 bushels per acre, Indian corn at 18 bushels, and
beans at 5.2 hundredweight per acre grossed income far below
that obtainable by harvesting and selling alfalfa.

In 1952 Fruitlanders sold 80,000 bales of hay which averaged
about 50 pounds each. Three baling machines owned by
Navahos did most of the packaging, which, at 16 cents per
bale, cost Fruitlanders a total of some $12,800. Besides the
tractor driver and machinery operator, who worked for 4 cents
per bale, a minimum of three other persons were employed—
one to feed the machine, one to tie the bales, and one to help
feed or tie as required. At 2.4 tons, or 96 50-pound bales, to the
acre, the baling of the 960 bales from ten acres required about
9½ days of work for three helpers and one equipment operator.
When one of the helpers was the farmer himself, his net profit
averaged $294 for his assignment. (See Table 3.)

Table 3. Average net profit from ten acres of alfalfa

Yield	24 tons (or 960 bales, 50 lb./bale) at $25.00/ton	$600.00
Baling cost	960 bales at $.16/bale 153.60	
Labor cost	Operator at $.04/bale 38.40	
	Two helpers, 9½ days at $6.00/day ... 114.00	306.00
	Net profit	$294.00

Now that the vehicular bridge made crossing the San Juan
River possible, some Fruitlanders hired non-Navahos to bale
their hay. Since automatic machines did not require extra labor,
they saved money; but the automatic machine did not tie the
bales adequately, and accordingly the traders did not pay the
full market price.

According to government estimates, there was little change
in the gross income of the assignees between 1949 and 1952. (See

Table 4.) Because of increased labor cost, however, the net returns for 1952 can be estimated as considerably less.

Table 4. Comparison of gross farm income of Fruitland farmers, 1949–1952

	$500 or less	$501–$1,000	$1,001–$1,500	$1,500 and over
1949	41%	45%	12%	2%
1952	43%	43%	13%	1%

Income from livestock, which at one time constituted the principal means of livelihood for Navahos, was very low between 1950 and 1952. In 1950 the livestock count in District 13 revealed that some 11,000 sheep units were on the range, less than the normal carrying capacity of about 16,000. A year later the government agent estimated that the number had dropped by another 3,000 sheep units, continuing a trend begun in 1944. (See Tables 5 and 6.)

Table 5. Number of families in District 13 without sheep, 1944–1952

Year	No. in Dist. 13	No. without sheep	% without sheep
1944	325	153	47.0%
1945	330	164	49.7
1947	345	170	49.2
1948	355	180	50.7
1950	380	219	57.6
1952	394	242	61.4

Table 6. Number of families in District 13 with sheep, 1944–1950 *

	Number of sheep			
Year	1–20	21–50	51–150	151 and more
1944	33	61	52	26
1945	54	77	40	15
1947	56	54	48	15
1948	56	54	27	15
1950	49	62	36	5

* Figures for 1952 are not available.

Another change in the economy of some Fruitlanders was brought about by the increase in welfare aid. About 10 per cent of Fruitland families received partial or total aid in 1953.[8] Since policy forbade aid to persons with sheep or with farm assignments, many aged farmers unable to work their farms adequately, and in need of help, did not request assistance. Some of these, however, received aid for their dependent children and grandchildren. Of fifteen persons about whom the writer secured specific data, the aid ranged from $9.50 to $120.00 per month, with the average $57.40, in addition to any other income.

Patterns of expenditure changed with the general rise in income. Fruitlanders no longer bought primarily at trading posts but purchased many items in town. Yet thirty-three employed Navahos, selected at random, spent an average of $96.43 per month or 43 per cent of their earned income at the trading post on foodstuffs, gas and oil, and clothing. The figure represents some cash advances against pay checks but not payment of back debts, which in some cases were considerable.

Thus although Fruitlanders spent more money in town than earlier, the traders received considerable business, for they continued to perform a variety of functions. For many Navahos they were middlemen. They paid fines for Navahos who were arrested and acted as financial managers for many Fruitland families. They cashed the laborers' checks and deducted what was owed them. In many cases the traders carried the regular payments on cars when Fruitlanders were temporarily unemployed, and they also advanced cash to the laborers. When the employed Navahos were delinquent in paying debts, however, it was not unusual for traders to impound their cars.

[8] William H. Kelly, *Indians of the Southwest* (First Annual Report, Bureau of Ethnic Research, Department of Anthropology, University of Arizona, 1953), p. 91, shows that for the reservation as a whole a little over 20 per cent received such aid.

Fruitlanders spent some of their new income wisely. They improved their housing, ate more, and clothed themselves better. By buying trucks and cars, they could commute to work, find work more easily, and shop where prices were lowest. Other expenditures were less practical. Some built shacks from expensive milled lumber. Many spent large amounts on soda pop, candy, and liquor. Some purchased cars which needed frequent repairs, often missed work because of motor troubles, and on days when they did not work made frequent trips into town, sometimes drinking and driving with disastrous results. Some, indeed, spent more on maintaining their cars than they did on food.

The sudden increase in the number of motor vehicles is dramatically illustrated by extracts from fieldworkers' notebooks. In July, 1949, a fieldworker wrote in her journal after attending a squaw dance, "There were wagons from Shiprock, Huerfano, and Burnhams. Many of the wagons had stayed the full time and there were a lot of people. The majority of the wagons were covered or plain types. Ours was the only passenger car for quite a while. Several pickup trucks came later." Fifteen months later, another student reporting a squaw dance held at the same place indicated that "cars, trucks, and pickup trucks had encircled the squaw-dance ground." Whereas before 1950 Fruitlanders owned 10 motor vehicles, all pickup trucks, within four months after the gas company came into the area 50 owned motor vehicles; by the summer of 1952 there were over 150 cars and trucks. Many individuals bought more than one car. Some Fruitlanders wrecked one and purchased a second, or defaulted on one and began payments on another; but the turnover can be attributed largely to other factors such as the high upkeep on old cars and the emergence of the motor vehicle as a prestige item, replacing the horse. Typically, the laborer purchased an old pickup truck for a few hundred dollars, made his payments, at once turned in the old car as down payment on a newer model, continued payments until he could turn in the second car as down payment on a third, and so on. Since Navahos were required to complete their installments within three to six months on lower-priced cars, payments were high.

Besides the initial outlay and regular payments, repairs were expensive. The sandy, rocky, high-centered roads, together with some lack of driving skill and neglect of maintenance, caused more than average wear. The high centers struck the oil pans, sometimes causing leakage of oil from the motor. Front ends and tie rods were often so badly damaged that driving became perilous. The washboard roads jarred body parts loose. In the summer sharp-pointed rocks broke tire casings, and in winter the frozen ground increased the hazard.

For example, Carl Yazzie, a war veteran, paid $600 for an early postwar model Ford. Soon he damaged two tires. Next, in extricating the car from sand he wore out the clutch and overheated and impaired the motor. After he spent about $65 to get his car repaired, a short circuit in the electrical system ignited the gas fumes, and the motor caught on fire. He managed to extinguish the fire with sand. But in doing so he threw sand into the crankcase because the oil-breather cap was missing. The cost of repairs was $178.50. Three months later, when cold weather arrived, he forgot to drain the water from the radiator and cracked the block. A rebuilt motor cost him $150.[9]

Another major, increased item of expense was recreation, including attendance at fiestas, Navaho and county fairs, and squaw dances,[10] as well as liquor and the resulting fines for drunken driving and disorderly conduct. When the Fruitlanders acquired motor vehicles, they drove not only to Farmington or

[9] For other instances of Fruitlanders' car troubles, see narratives of Slim Ford and Junior Begay in Chapter X.

[10] The writer must perhaps make clear that he does not include in "recreation" the cost of participating in or contributing to ceremonials.

to Shiprock but to Gallup and to Durango, Colorado, both nearly three hours away. Some even drove the 300 miles to Flagstaff. On such trips they purchased extra quantities of fuel, ate in restaurants, and slept at hotels or camped out.

On weekends and before attending squaw dances and fiestas, they borrowed heavily from traders. It was not unusual to spend $30 to $40 in a few days. Before repeal of the law which prohibited sale of intoxicants to Indians, Fruitlanders purchased pint bottles of wine from bootleggers at $3 and quarts at $5. Purchases of three or four pints or two quarts were frequent, and arrests for disturbing the peace or for driving while drunk became numerous. After repeal, sale or consumption on the reservation was still prohibited, so bootlegging continued. Some Navaho bootleggers estimated that they earned between $75 and $100 at weekend squaw dances.

Alcohol was one source of release from tensions. Because of the Project's position on the border of the reservation and close to town, there were perhaps more opportunities for Fruitland Navahos to obtain liquor than for others who lived farther away. Repeal of the liquor law made wine available at less than half the price formerly paid bootleggers. High wages after 1950 made liquor all the more accessible. Under its influence, latent hostility emerged into the open in acts of violence.

Tabulation of arrests and fines reported in the local newspaper, before and after repeal, reveals that a significant part of some Navaho incomes was paid to Farmington and tribal police courts. During one month the total fines collected by the Farmington police court totaled over $1,000.

Possession of cars facilitated frequent trips into town by members of the family as well. With cash in their pockets, Fruitlanders went to department and five-and-dime stores and purchased ready-made blouses and skirts, saddle shoes, and sweaters. Even the less-acculturated women often purchased these, and the men bought low-cut shoes, boots, and other items which they could not find at trading posts.

As gas-company workers moved westward with the advance of the pipeline, trading posts sold many tents. Many families improved their permanent dwellings with window frames, glass windows, doors, wooden floors, asphalt roofing, and paint. New cast-iron stoves, radios, and a variety of "gadgets" were acquired.

Medical expenses increased for some. The number of native curing rites sponsored by Fruitlanders declined in the fall of 1950 and in 1951 but increased again in 1952. Although sings were held during the peak of the gas-line activity, attendance was not as great as in the past because men did not wish to be absent from work; in 1952, accordingly, most squaw dances and sings were held on weekends.

In 1951 Fruitlanders held the first *Yeibichei* or the Night Way chant since 1933, and a second was held the following year. The expenses involved in holding these ceremonials were great, for not only were singers brought from the Black Mesa and Crystal area, nearly a hundred miles away, but dance teams came from various parts of the reservation. Each participant was paid and fed during the nine days of the ceremony. Only through wide support of wage earners were these sings possible.

A very small group of Fruitlanders made investments. Some, like Joe Bitsilly, worked for the gas company to replenish herds depleted in the drought. Others purchased permits in the hope of some day becoming livestock operators. The Frank James family, with two wageworkers grossing over $600 a month, purchased 200 head early in 1952 and another hundred head in 1953. Ned Garwood, already the owner of over 200 head of sheep, bought out several permittees.

Another form of investment was farm machinery. By 1952

Fruitlanders owned eight tractors, four hay baling machines, and a number of new implements such as hay rakes, cultivators, and plows. To obtain implements Fruitlanders borrowed money when possible from the Tribal Revolving Loan Fund, repaying the loan with interest. In April, 1953, about sixteen Fruitlanders were making such payments: two on an original loan of $2,000 or more; two on amounts between $1,600 and $1,700; and the remainder on less than $600. Two college boys borrowed a total of $1,100. Eleven were delinquent by amounts varying between 32 cents and $1,627.46. Of $11,662.10 originally borrowed, an unpaid balance of $4,770.43 remained. An examination of the list of borrowers revealed that ten held jobs with the government, in town, or on the gas line; three were livestock men; two had no income other than from their farms; one person's occupation was unknown; and one received regular compensation from the Veterans' Administration.

CHAPTER VIII

Emergence of a New Order

THE availability of wagework in the vicinity of the Fruitland Project influenced all aspects of social life of The People. What happened in the San Juan Valley was a concentrated form of the same changes taking place elsewhere on the reservation. The major issue appeared to be a choice of the direction which The People would take—the white or the Navaho way. Although Fruitlanders as individuals and in their groupings had long been interlocked with forces outside their Irrigation Project, they themselves failed to recognize such relationships and deliberately limited their direct participation in the world outside. But after 1950 they too saw economic acceleration in the American Southwest and their own part therein.

They were not wholly prepared to gear themselves into the rapidly changing social and economic environment. They made some adjustments, but their very prosperity and the major shifts in orientation which might help them make further adjustments in the wider society created serious disturbances. Because they were ill-prepared, the Fruitlanders were unable to make adaptations and adjustments rapidly enough to keep up with the overpowering rate of change to which they were exposed.

Out of this chaos emerged a strange, incongruous blend of white and Navaho ways, a blend not always satisfactory or coherent but nevertheless serviceable as a temporary cushion during transition. Tribal leadership, for example, had on the one hand become highly organized in order that The People might benefit from exploitation of reservation resources by private enterprises. On the other hand, because of this bureaucracy (and a variety of communication difficulties), the leaders had acquired so much more knowledge of the modern world than most Navahos that a serious gap was created between the two. So too at Fruitland: experiences in off-reservation work and in the more immediate employment market affected the local political structure, and factions based upon special interest and new orientation emerged.

Reorientation in the Fruitlanders' way of life was perhaps most vividly seen in the enthusiasm that they showed toward education for their children. Education was now considered a "cure-all" and a sure means to success. (Sending children to school was also one method of feeding them, now that they no longer contributed to the immediate economic needs of the family, and also of freeing parents for off-reservation jobs.) Nevertheless, education for a time introduced new confusion. Faced by widely divergent social and economic cultural environments, the children learned to behave like non-Navahos in the company of hundreds of other Navaho children; then upon returning home they found little or no home life of either the traditional or the non-Navaho kind.

Nearby wagework similarly affected Navaho religious life. The older Fruitlanders worried over the lack of interest shown by younger adults and children. Eventually a large segment of the Navaho population may lose most or all knowledge of traditional ceremonies—or perhaps, in a new situation and atmosphere, revive them.

This chapter will detail the effects of wagework on three

aspects of life in Fruitland: (1) tribal and local political systems, (2) education, and (3) Navaho religion. One new social relationship, too, must be explored—that with large-scale regular employers and with one's fellow employees. Effects on family life will be presented in the following chapter.

Previous to 1950, irregular employment had served to excuse Navahos' failure to understand rigid schedules and technical skills. The white man's pace was often as slow as that of the Navahos, and employers were willing to make some concessions when ceremonials were held. Since there was never a labor surplus in the San Juan Valley, farmers had no recourse but to wait until the Navahos were ready to work.

But in the major shift of economic base after 1950, the new employers showed little appreciation for Navaho behavior; if the Navaho wished to acquire a cash income, he had to adjust his schedule to that of his employer. For a while, as construction work accelerated and the demand for labor exceeded the labor supply, Navahos were lax in conforming to employers' expectations; if discharged, they could find employment elsewhere. But in time irresponsible action, especially on the part of a few young men, hurt the Navahos' opportunities for moving into jobs which involved learning new skills.

Immediately following 1950 the wagework pace was vigorous. Work was readily available and the hours were long and arduous. Whereas most Navahos adhered to schedules and worked diligently, some preferred to quit after the second or third pay check. (Two pay checks at this time equaled a season's income from the farm.) Others, through lack of understanding of the subtleties of white ways or because differences were not explained either to the white employees or to Navahos, developed negative attitudes. *The Pipeliner*, official publication of the gas company, had stated in the fall of 1950:

The Navahos who have taken jobs with the construction crews are doing a sterling job. They are quick to learn, hard working, ambitious. Many of them have worked into skilled or semi-skilled classification. Quite a few are dozer operators; others operate other types of machines. To watch these men hustle today, you would think that they had been working at their jobs for many years.

Two years later a company official expressed a belief that Navahos were inflexible and reluctant to take jobs which required the learning of complex skills or additional responsibilities, preferring work which required repetition and precision. "If you would tell a Navaho to put in some stakes in a straight line to make a fence, he would never ask you any questions—he would go right ahead and put in a fence that was straighter than any white man can do." But, he said, Navahos left machinery unattended during changes in work shifts without notifying the foreman, thus exposing men on incoming shifts to possible injuries and machinery to damage. "All they knew was that when twelve o'clock came their time was up, and off they went for their hogans."

Employers considered, too, that Navaho labor was expensive —that they must hire 10 per cent more Navahos because some would quit without notice or arrive at work drunk. The Navahos themselves soon perceived that they were acquiring a bad reputation, as one remarked:

Some Indian boys work a few days and then quit. Some of them get drunk and do all kinds of things like that. The first thing you know all of the bosses say that the Indians are no good for work and it's hard for us that have families to get a job. They think that if some do, we all do.

When by 1953 many of the big construction jobs were completed and non-Navahos from all over the Southwest began to move into the San Juan Valley, the same Navaho remarked on the difficulty of securing employment: "They used to have lots of jobs in town—they were pretty easy to get. Now this year it's tough to get jobs. It's hard to get jobs since a lot of people moved in from Texas. So we Indians lose the jobs."

The companies which hired large numbers of Navahos attempted to treat them on an equal basis with their other employees, but lack of careful explanation sometimes resulted in misunderstanding. For example, although gas-company officials believed that they could have hired Navahos for much less pay, they adhered to their policy of paying comparable wages for comparable work. Still many Navahos felt that they were being cheated, largely because management failed to explain paycheck deductions for taxes and unemployment insurance.

Some personal antagonisms also arose on the job. A foreman with one construction company complained that Navahos kept almost completely to themselves and did not interact with the rest of the employees. Some bosses and white workers felt that Navahos thought themselves too good to mix with the rest: "They look down on everyone who is not Navaho—they are a proud people." Others did not wish to sleep in the same bunkhouses or ride in the same trucks with Navahos, saying they were dirty.

Faced with language difficulties and struck by many cultural differences, the Navahos learned without benefit of established patterns. Those who spoke no English relied upon the advice of Navahos who did, and they faced many situations in which they must go the "white way" without guidance. They were taken to physicians and to hospitals for examinations and treatments. They ate in restaurants. They took showers and changed their clothes more frequently than on the reservation because of complaints from fellow workers. For such situations they had to seek explanations, often inadequate, from their English-speaking Navaho companions.

Beginning in 1949, one of the principal objectives of Navajo Service superintendents was to carry out an intensive program of self-determination among members of the Tribal Council. In order to gain The People's respect, councilmen had to be made aware of their increasing responsibilities for tribal welfare and to participate more fully in the administration of rehabilitation programs. Within three years extraordinary changes were effected. Members and officers were now nominated by special committees and by conventions and elected by the secret ballot.[1] Tribal judges were elected, not appointed by the Indian Bureau. An advisory committee of eleven council members, including the tribal chairman and vice-chairman, assumed so many executive duties and responsibilities that it was almost continuously in session. Permanent committees, long barred by The People's mistrust for delegation of authority, were created to study resources, community services, engineering, general administration, reservation trading, and tribal loans. In 1950 the tribe moved its official headquarters from Shiprock to Window Rock, expanded its permanent staff from 4 to 23 (27 in 1954), and created a tribal organization for handling some of the responsibilities of the Indian Bureau.[2] By 1952 there was a move to reactivate the chapters in order to renovate tribal organization at the "grass roots." These were major changes and would probably have been impossible but for the social and economic cli-

---

[1] Revision of election procedures in the election of council delegates included the following, as stated in *Revised Procedures for the Election of Council officers, Delegates, and Judges in the Navajo Tribal Court of Indian Offense, Approved by Council in Regular Session on September 15, 1950*, printed at the Phoenix Indian School, Dec., 1950, p. 3: (1) registration of voters; (2) the secret ballot; (3) absentee registration and vote for off-reservation employed Navahos; (4) the selection of their own running mates by nominees for the office of tribal chairman; (5) the election of judges for the tribal courts.

Broader implications were summarized in a paragraph found in the same *Revised Procedures*, p. 2: "Today the Navaho people have the right to vote alongside other American citizens in state and national elections. To teach them the techniques involved in such elections, as well as to make tribal elections orderly and systematic, a ballot system adapted to the present day needs of the Navaho people has been incorporated."

[2] *Planning in Action on the Navajo-Hopi Indian Reservations*, Report no. 2, 1952, pp. 45, 47, 50.

mate of the time and the remarkable skills of the Indian Service superintendents involved.

The streamlining of council structure enabled it to function effectively at the tribal though not at the local level. Whereas the delegates had earlier spent much time at council meetings presenting individual constituents' problems and individuals' losses due to stock reduction, now the emphasis was on reservation-wide decisions: tribal enterprise, drought-relief loans, and the use of tribal resources. (Symbolically, delegates' expenses were no longer met by local collections.) After 1950, the Council became a governing body much like that of a large corporation, with a budget of over $1,000,000 in 1954.[3] By 1958 the tribal budget had increased to over $14,000,000. Its negotiations with firms extracting natural resources from tribal land involved several million dollars, and it managed tribal enterprises with a gross income of $3,500,000.[4]

But although the Council spent many weeks each year coping with tribal affairs and participating in the administration of tribal and government programs, there was little communication with The People generally. In the period between December 1, 1950, and January 31, 1951, a total of 311 eligible voters registered to vote in Fruitland's two election communities, 152 from Upper Fruitland (Unit 1 and vicinity) and 159 from Lower Fruitland (Units 2 and 3 and vicinity).[5] In Upper Fruitland 50 of 87 farm assignees registered, or 57 per cent, as against only 40 of 123, or 33 per cent, in Lower Fruitland. Most assignees from Lower Fruitland were working for the gas company and traveling southwestward during this time; therefore the registration figures were notably low.

On January 7, 1951, local conventions were held to select

[3] *Ibid.*, p. 50.
[4] *The Navajo Yearbook*, Report no. 4, Fiscal Year 1957, p. 123.
[5] Figures from registration lists and election returns.

election judges and to nominate council delegates from each of the two election communities. In Upper Fruitland one of the candidates nominated for delegate spoke English and one did not; in Lower Fruitland, the incumbent, who spoke no English, opposed two candidates who did. At the same conventions, representatives were elected to attend the provincial convention to be held at Shiprock to nominate a candidate for tribal chairman. On March 6 and 7 those who had registered cast their ballots. At each of the two polling places one government representative and two election judges were present. As each registrant entered the polling station (the schoolhouse for Lower Fruitland, a private residence for Upper Fruitland), his attention was directed to the sample ballot posted on the wall. The judges then called the registrant to the table in the center of the room, where he was asked for his registration slip. When the matching slip was found, a ballot was placed on the table before the registrant, with pictures of the candidates as well as their names, and he was instructed in detail to vote for one council candidate, for one pair of nominees for chairman and vice-chairman of the Council, and for each of five candidates (only five were nominated) for judge in the tribal courts.[6]

Although election judges and government representatives explained the procedure in great detail, many voters re-examined the sample ballot. When the judges noted that the voters

[6] Of the seven candidates for the five judgeships, two withdrew. Therefore, the election judges instructed each voter to cast his vote for each of the candidates, without exception. When the judges examined the results for each of the communities, they found that the voters in Lower Fruitland consistently failed to follow instructions. The voters had cast their ballots only for the candidate who was to occupy the office for the northeastern part of the reservation, but not for the four others. Interviews with the election judges and with a few selected voters revealed that the voters did not understand the instructions and that they had voted for the judge for their particular area—the only important one because, they believed, he would be the one to try them should they ever have to appear in court.

hesitated in entering the voting booth, one or the other judge accompanied the voter into the booth to repeat the instructions on procedure. The completed ballots were placed in a locked metal box.

Voting was heavy. Ninety-six per cent of the registrants in Upper Fruitland and 90 per cent of the registrants in Lower Fruitland cast ballots. Of the two incumbent delegates, John Rogers was defeated in Upper Fruitland and Mr. Red House, in Lower Fruitland, won only a bare majority, 77 of the 145 votes cast; 32 voters marked their ballots for his opponents, and 36 did not vote for any of the three candidates.[7]

The Fruitlanders' conception of their social world was reflected in the way they voted; that is, they cast ballots only for those persons who they felt were closely linked with their own life. Fruitlanders displayed little interest in electing candidates for the offices of chairman, vice-chairman, and tribal judges. For the office of tribal chairman, most Fruitlanders voted for the candidate from the neighboring district, whom many had seen at various local ceremonial and social affairs.

Although the secret ballot enabled the Fruitlanders to participate in the election of tribal officers and their local representatives, the gap between the grass roots and the Council widened. The councilmen spent much time at meetings at Window Rock,[8] and the people themselves were too busily engaged in wagework to attend local meetings even when they were announced. There were new responsibilities for which neither the

[7] It is the writer's guess that one reason why some did not vote for delegates was their misunderstanding of the balloting procedures. Fruitlanders who were interviewed immediately after the election stated that they felt that, should the elected official find out that their votes went to the opposition, they would stand little chance of getting recommendations for loans or assignments.

[8] The delegates attended 13 lengthy council sessions between 1951 and 1953, and the delegates on the Advisory Committee attended 47 additional meetings.

people nor their leaders were ready. Since neither models nor clarification of the expected behavioral patterns had been established for the grass roots, each unit at Fruitland reacted to the changing political situation in a different manner. The unit most strongly resembling the old social organization began to disintegrate while that most acculturated became better integrated.

Since most gas-company employees came from units 2 and 3, they were more regularly absent from chapter meetings than were Unit 1 residents. When Fruitland as a whole held an election for chapter officers in 1951, the majority of those attending were again from Unit 1, and Ned Garwood and Joe Benally from that unit were elected president and vice-president. Ray Johnson of Unit 2, the outgoing president, received the third highest number of votes and was elected secretary-treasurer.

Ray stated that he should continue as president, because Ned Garwood spoke, read, and wrote English and so could better fill the office of secretary-treasurer. Although Unit 2 residents present at the meeting were few, they insisted on Ray Johnson's proposal to rearrange the election results. Accordingly, Unit 1 residents decided to reactivate their own chapter, a move they had contemplated for fifteen years but hesitated to do because of social pressures from Unit 2. Now they lost no time in nominating and electing their own officers.

Both leading candidates for the presidency of the new chapter spoke English. The younger candidate, though only in his twenties, was generally considered one of the best-educated persons in this unit, with a real command of English and, reputedly, a far larger Navaho vocabulary than most Fruitlanders who knew Navaho only; moreover, he was familiar with the details of numerous Navaho curing chants.[9] Unfortunately,

[9] The writer had learned from the young candidate, when bringing him back from a council meeting at Window Rock some months earlier, that while attending a Santa Fe public school he had written a term paper on

he was soon afterward called for service in the armed forces.

His opponent, Lawrence Willie, a man about forty-five years of age, had had only three years of formal education but, having grown up in a non-Indian community, spoke excellent English. He had held numerous positions with the government and with private contractors. He came to Fruitland as a laborer when work began on the canal and was one of the first to acquire an assignment. At a time when most Fruitlanders still built hogans on their farms, he constructed an adobe house like those across the river. Following wartime service, he worked for the government but was soon discharged. His neighbors in Unit 1 now considered his facility in English enough of an asset to outweigh some of his weaknesses, and they elected him president of the new chapter. Ned Garwood was elected secretary.

The people of Unit 1, long convinced that their problems were not shared by Unit 2, now attempted to meet them. One of the first issues raised was the need for a centrally located well. (In 1950 when meters were installed in town, the previous source of water for Unit 1 had been closed.) Lawrence Willie made efforts to secure help from the government and a missionary, but when, eighteen months later, the government dug a well, the water was saline and unpalatable.

The distribution of irrigation water to farmers was another problem which the people of Unit 1 undertook to solve under Lawrence Willie's leadership. During meetings with farmers along different irrigation laterals, chapter officers stressed the necessity of scheduling the limited supply of water and insisted that the old excuse for nonadherence, a sing or a squaw dance, was no longer valid since most farmers now had cars and re-

---

Navaho curing rites. The literature so interested him, he said, that he had spent considerable time studying it at the museum in the old Palace of the Governor.

turned to their homes after each night's performance. The farmers worked out a detailed plan for each of the laterals, and through two seasons there were few complaints of water shortage.

Unit 1 could not acquire the semblance of a formally organized community without changes in other attitudes. Older Navahos grew more tolerant of those in the middle-age range. When the gas company recruited primarily from traditionalistic Unit 2, there was an easing in Unit 1 of social pressure against government workers. But while Unit 1 showed signs of becoming integrated, Unit 2 began to lose its cohesion. The absence from the area, during waking hours, of most able-bodied men created a community of females, aged men, and younger children; of the three men remaining who had been active politically, only the present councilman remained so, and he divided his time between duties at Window Rock and catching up on delayed farm chores. The chapter president, normally responsible for calling meetings, worked for the gas company. Neither tribal nor government policies could be adequately communicated. Local self-determination deteriorated, as three case histories will show.

In 1950 livestock owners were concerned about the range. Two years of drought had caused many livestock owners to sell out, and of those who remained in business many were concerned about the excess, unbranded horses which roamed at large. One group asked tribal and chapter officials to authorize a sale and, together with the supervisor, developed a plan. Local leaders obtained government money for a roundup, and the supervisor got in touch with a buyer. Within a week, over fifty horses were corralled. But when tribal and chapter officials announced a date for the sale at a squaw dance, small groups gathered to state their objections. The following day the supervisor and the buyer waited at the corral until noon, but no one appeared. The supervisor and the buyer went to look for the chapter officials but could not find them. When they returned to the corral, they discovered that someone had turned the horses loose.

Although the effort failed, the government was for once not the scapegoat. Rather, hostility became focused on the livestock owners, and the members of this special-interest group tightened their own associations.

A second failure in self-determination concerned care for the needy. When surplus commodities were made available, the supervisor, together with the welfare worker and local officials, selected a committee to handle distribution. Announcements were made of the distribution dates. But through some misunderstanding families who came in trucks and cars were given all the foodstuffs. When the poor arrived in wagons and on foot, there was little left. An informal check revealed that the more affluent took 75 per cent of the commodities, leaving little for the indigents. Although Navaho responsibility in commodity distribution was the goal, the goal was still far away; the supervisor and the welfare worker arranged the next distribution through a closely supervised committee to insure that persons listed as welfare cases received aid.

A third experiment in local self-determination concerned tribal loans, made (until 1953) on the basis of need, ability to make payments, and the recommendations of agency personnel and local councilmen. The Council Committee on Loans made the final decision. No clear picture was given to applicants of the procedures, the source of funds, or their responsibility for payments. When installments became due, government employees informed the borrower and made attempts to collect. Often those who were delinquent became hostile not only toward collecting agents, but to government programs generally. Many applicants, informed that they could not borrow because they had not yet repaid loans made to them between 1929 and 1938, replied, "I don't remember ever borrowing this money," or "I will pay some on this account in a few days." [10] No community attempt to help with collections or to explain their necessity ever had an important effect on the Fruitlanders' attitude toward loans and their repayment.

The People themselves realized that their lives were undergoing some sort of transformation, but because their socioculture was not completely geared to the new situation, they still had not developed a social organization or skills to handle new problems. Although their intention was to mesh their orientation with that of the white pattern, the means for learning to act in the new situation were imperfect, and they have tended sometimes to respond either in the pattern familiar to them or at random.

Reorientation of their values toward the white way was reflected especially in the Navahos' new effort to secure education for their children. Educational opportunities for Navaho children have always been a principal issue at council meetings. The federal-Navaho treaty ratified in 1868 specified that the government should build a schoolhouse and furnish one teacher for each thirty children. This provision was not always appreciated by the Indians nor honored by the government. The Navahos, as well as the government, were responsible for failures to develop a satisfactory educational system.

In 1946 there were facilities for about 5,000 of some 24,000 children of school age.[11] When Navahos demanded new school buildings, government officials replied that until present schools became crowded (many schools had closed in the mid-1940's, for lack of attendance) Congress would not appropriate money for new buildings. It was not until 1950 that large numbers of Navahos began attending Indian Service schools. Registration and attendance were no longer "up to the children." By 1952–

---

[10] Abstracts of Extension Service Report, 1946.
[11] Kelly, *Indians of the Southwest*, pp. 81–88.

1953, 13,767 children (of some 27,065 of school age) were receiving formal education.[12]

At Fruitland, some 170 smaller children were enrolled in 1951 in the local day and boarding school. In 1952 a bus transported about thirty children who wished to attend on a daily basis. This was a pilot attempt to determine whether the entire Fruitland educational plant could be converted from a boarding to a full-time day school. If the parents accepted the transition, fifty additional pupils could be accommodated by replacing dormitories with classroom equipment.

After the vehicular bridge was completed and parents could drive them to school on the way to work, some thirty Fruitland children regularly attended the state public school. The walk home from the bridge or the sometimes long wait for a ride was a hardship especially during the winter months. Now the more acculturated parents asked and were soon granted Indian Service transportation for state public as well as federal school children. The next year the public school bus traveled the length of Unit 1.

Beginning in 1946, those twelve years of age and older who had never attended schools were encouraged to enter institutions in Oklahoma, New Mexico, Arizona, Utah, Oregon, California, and Nevada. In 1952, 4,709 Navaho children, of whom about 600 were regular students, attended these schools, and by 1955 off-reservation boarding school enrollment had increased to 6,499.[13] Some parents who objected to off-reservation schools had opportunities to visit them when engaged in wagework nearby and were impressed with what they saw. Formerly school authorities had visited families and attempted to persuade them to enroll their children. After 1950 parents

[12] *Ibid.*
[13] *Planning in Action on the Navajo-Hopi Indian Reservations,* Report no. 3, 1953, p. 5.

competed to enroll their children. Resistance to boarding schools failed to develop even though most were regulated and institutional in pattern. In general, children looked forward to returning to the campus, and some elected to remain away from their homes during the summer, working at school or nearby towns.

Increased wagework opportunities did not decrease the number of sings held, except for a few months after the gas company first began to hire Fruitlanders. Some singers claimed that they had to perform more rites than formerly in part because population had increased and in part because younger men and women did not want to become singers.

I have more than twice as many sings now as five years ago. This year [1951] I don't go out to look for people to hold prayers and ceremonies. They come to me; and I don't want to refuse any of them because it is just a song and prayer for two days and two nights. In the early days there were fewer hogans, and so there were fewer sings. In ten to fifteen years, there will not be a medicine man because the boys are not learning it. I am one of the medicine men, my father and grandfather were too. It has been going on from one generation to another. . . . If white doctor doesn't work, then they [patients] should come back to the medicine man.

At the same time, Fruitlanders readily accepted some of the white man's medical facilities. By 1950 most pregnant women attended prenatal clinics. The gas company insisted that health was something more than merely "feeling good," and its own doctor examined truckload after truckload of applicants. Some passed; others, put on the waiting list until their afflictions responded to treatment, were soon employed. Once at work, they visited the doctor for "shots" lest sickness prevent them from working. The company doctor had such an excellent reputation that many Navahos were willing to pay him rather than get free services at the mission or government clinic.

Although visits to white doctors did not imply that sings were no longer necessary for a complete cure, Navahos now felt that sings did not have the same religious significance as formerly. They said that people had forgotten how to behave at sings and acted "kind of crazy." Declared Christians retained a firm belief in native rituals but not as now practiced. The scheduling of ceremonies over weekends was, after all, hardly compatible with the accepted white pattern of Saturday-night relaxation. The ideal pattern at sings was for all participants to contribute toward the ceremony by refraining from all misconduct. Now deviant behavior, common enough even before 1950, became almost inevitable, sometimes even among the singers themselves.

Charley Begay and Joe Pete came in. They were both obviously drunk because they had a hard time talking. Charley Begay pushed Pinto Whitehorse aside and sat between him and the medicine man. Little Mexican, the sponsor, seemed to be embarrassed by the presence of the drunkards. Charley Begay tried to sing but he only uttered croaking sounds. He waited a little while and then took a fifth of rye whiskey from underneath his shirt and offered the singer a drink. The singer took a shot. Then Charley Begay offered it to the second medicine man who also sipped out a little. Three of the men went outside where they continued to drink, and they seemed to enjoy themselves because they laughed loudly.[14]

Members of the tribal police force attended most large ceremonials. On several occasions sings had to be discontinued because the policemen jailed members of the participating families for drunkenness.

At the two *Yeibichei* rites held at Fruitland in 1952 and 1953, the sponsors each day collected the wine bottles thrown away the preceding night. A man of sixty-eight observed:

[14] Several days later one of the medicine men observed: "You saw those people going outside. They drank all night. That man gave me some to drink, but I drank just a little. When they try to give me too much, I don't drink it. The medicine won't work if I drink too much. I sure like to drink sometimes but I stay at home when I do so people won't see me."

In those old days when they had *Yeibichei* they weren't supposed to take whiskey. The six dancers ain't suppose to drink. Even those who had sores weren't supposed to dance. The children were not supposed to see the dance except during the day—after they see it four times then they are given a mask to see through it. Then they can see the dance at night time. The kids are in line and each kid sees through this mask. On the next day they look through the mask. But nowadays they don't keep it up. The kids just go look at the dance without first looking through the mask. It is supposed to cause deafness and blindness. Now it is different, I guess, because people are increasing, and the grandchildren are not told about it.

Now the dancers and the medicine men are half drunk. In the old days they didn't allow that because mistakes would cause sickness to take [all the people in] the area where they are having the sing. . . . They say that it ain't right to use liquor . . . because it causes sickness. Twelve dancers from over the mountain knew how to dance in perfect order all night long. Now when they try to get together, one man, two men, would not be around because they would be drunk, and they can't dance together.

The same man explained some medicine men's drinking as an indirect result of stock reduction and the Navahos' lack of sheep. In the old days, he said,

there was plenty of mutton to give the medicine man and helpers. They would be proud of it and they did it [rites] right up to the last day. Now, when the medicine man sees no mutton, just coffee and bread, they don't care for that, so they start drinking and don't care. The helpers are the ones who won't stay with it if there ain't enough to eat.

In commenting on earlier behavior another elderly man was even more critical of the new age. He said, "They never let no white man come around. They were strict. Now any tramp could come around to see. They wouldn't let a drunken man dance, or even let a drunken man come to the sing."

But although the Navahos had accepted hospitals and modern

medicine and deplored the conditions under which curing rites were performed, they still held firm to the belief that native religious ceremonies were necessary. A singer explained the reason for this.

We get sick, sometimes out of coyote, dogs, lizards, and anything like that; some of them get lightning strike, but the doctor doesn't know anything about that. They just know what is happening inside, and can cut, but they don't know anything about the other kind. So we have to have both kinds, white man's medicine, and sings. If there are no more medicine man I don't know what we are going to do.

When the end of sings come, they say that there will be a different way of life . . . and the end of the world anyway. If the sings stop, the people will live in a new way, like the white people.

CHAPTER IX

Navaho Families, Extended, Compressed, and Fractured

FRUITLAND families made varying adjustments to the changed situation, depending upon (1) the degree to which family members were able to vary their role behavior in response to the changing situation, (2) the isolation of the biological family or its position in a family grouping of some size and structure, and (3) the degree to which family members clarified their definition of situational changes, reference-group norms, and their own roles in the changing scene. In the case studies which follow this chapter, such factors will be shown as accounting for the differences of adjustments even by members of large extended families (such as Slim Ford, Harry, and Sam David in Little Ute's group and Hosteen Benally in Strong Man's outfit) or among relatively isolated Fruitlanders (such as Mike Cooper, Carl Jackson, and Lawrence Willie).

Whereas some changes in family life occurred before 1950 —because of shifts in residence patterns imposed by government assignment of new farms to men, because of off-reservation work, because of army experiences, and because of boarding schools for children—the traditional forms of behavior w highly considered though less and less adhered to. The basis for perpetuating this belief, however, was weaker the fact that school children had no opportunities to hear kinship terms or to observe kinship practices.[1]

Already in 1950 changes in role and status had brought about gains in power, prestige, and material advantage to some and losses to others.[2] Some roles had been weakened or even ceased to exist. New roles were often inadequately practiced—for example, the father's economic responsibility for his family in the new cash economy. Learning went on through trial and error.

In view of the government policy of assigning land to the male heads of families, it was necessary that husbands, wives, and unmarried children rely on each other for more and more social and emotional support. The husband and father, now the authoritative head of the household, controlled its finances. Whereas, in the past, a wife and her children were often supported by her family when the father left them for a time, today they were dependent almost entirely upon him. (Should a father choose to desert the family completely, the family would, however, be supported by welfare assistance.)

In imparting economic skills to his sons the father now had only a minor role. During the summer, to be sure, he might teach them farming and transfer all but the heavy work to them. But, having few sheep, he could give them little or no instruction in sheep raising. Schoolboys were more apt to receive vocational training at school, and youths not in school learned on the job. Then too, with his children at boarding

---

[1] Glen Fisher, in his *Directed Culture Change in Nayarit, Mexico* (Middle American Institute; New Orleans: Tulane University of Louisiana, 1953), p. 140, states that it would be theoretically possible to change culture in one generation if the socializing process could be quickly and radically altered.

[2] See Ralph Linton, ed., *Acculturation in Seven American Indian Tribes* (New York: D. Appleton–Century Co., 1950), p. 472.

school, the father no longer could transmit the "legends and myths about the ways of the gods and the moral order" during the winter months.[3]

The increased responsibility of the father, especially as primary economic provider, was something that he had only recently learned to exercise. During the war, when he left for railroad employment or the armed services, his family remained at home. He made little provision for their support since traditionally a man and wife were financially independent. He began to understand his role as provider in more concrete terms only after he was employed by the gas company. Living at home, he commuted daily to work. His wife assumed responsibility for household expenditures. Although he might refuse to tell her what he earned, she soon learned from others in the community. In many families, once the family-unit concept was understood, wives began to handle the money.

Until they controlled family spending, the position of the women had deteriorated considerably. For the wife and mother at Fruitland did not have the social and emotional support traditionally lent by her mother and other nearby female relatives. With her husband away and her children at school a large part of the time, her roles began to change. With neither sheep to herd nor wool to weave, she was no longer economically self-supporting. In the event of divorce or separation, she was the partner who must leave, for the assignment and the improvements on the farm belonged to the man. Whatever domestic instruction she might give her daughters conflicted with what they learned at school. With most foodstuffs purchased at the store, girls had fewer opportunities to learn how to prepare food in the traditional manner.

[3] See Solon T. Kimball and John H. Provinse, "Navaho Social Organization in Land Use Planning," *Applied Anthropology*, I (1942), 20–21, and Robert N. Rapoport, *Changing Navaho Religious Values* (Papers of the Peabody Museum of American Archaeology and Ethnology, Harvard University, vol. XLI, no. 2; Cambridge: The Museum, 1954), p. 73.

On the other hand, particularly after 1950, women participated more in the farm work. In the men's absence, they raised and harvested the crops. Some even stacked and loaded hay on trucks which they drove to the trading post. Profits from the field had always been shared by all family members, but the greater participation of the women in farming gave them a firmer hold on the investment.

The shift from the traditional matrilocal residence pattern to that of patrilocal or separate residence had certain disadvantages for the wife. More commonly now, a daughter-in-law lived with the husband's family in his absence. Besides the insecurity which she faced through being separated from her own kin, she was usually dominated by the husband's mother and had nothing similar to the "mother-in-law avoidance" that traditionally protected the young man living with his wife's people. Attached to her young children and with her relatives often unable to help her economically, she was largely controlled by the household of her husband. She could and did, however, leave for town employment. There money, shelter, and food were assured. If these were no substitute for the meaningful relationships of the traditional Navaho life, still employment might serve as an escape—and free access to sex experiences and liquor.

After spending most of the year at local and off-reservation boarding schools children were restless at home. Young boys and girls spent much of their free time in town. In some instances neither father nor mother could control them, in part because, through the winter, they were not economically dependent upon their parents. The maternal uncle, traditionally the disciplinarian, was rarely at hand. More important, the children had no work to do at home. Their participation in the new economic life was almost nonexistent. Older boys might still help on the farm, but if possible they preferred to work for wages. The smaller children, who a generation ago would have herded sheep, no longer had this task. During the summer school children got into difficulties. Their troubles were largely due to lack of supervision by their parents, who were themselves enmeshed in new complexities, and to the general lack of recreational outlets.

Upon their return from schools the children seemed less shy, and they restlessly asserted a kind of freedom which older Navahos never had in their Navaho-oriented society. Some old-timers were concerned lest the children forget Navaho ways. Most parents, however, could not redirect their children toward Navaho orientation because they themselves set poor examples.

Older boys rarely returned home at all but worked summers; adolescent girls too found jobs as maids or in cafes. Many of those children who did return home went into town. Unsupervised there, they roamed the streets or went to movies. Their behavior at squaw dances was similarly non-Navaho. Girls wore Western-style clothes, slacks, tight sweaters, and saddle shoes and addressed boys in English.

School children exhibited such behavior only during the summer, but adolescents not attending school engaged in these activities throughout the year. The boys walked around the town in gangs, drank, and fought among themselves or with Spanish-Americans. The hostility which they evidenced against their more acculturated brothers probably came in large part from their own off-reservation work experiences.

I never did like the way some of the "long-hairs" [traditional Navahos] were refused rooms in hotels. In one town where I was, they bought round trip tickets from Barstow on the Greyhound. The Greyhound driver kept turning these men out to let the white people on. I told these men to hang on to me. The bus-driver said that there was only one seat for me. I refused it. I told him that I had two men with me and I couldn't go without them. Then the bus driver said that he would let them stand although there were vacant seats on the bus. I stood with them for about 100 miles. I have done this more than once.

Harvest season off the reservation provided opportunities for sexual license. Boys frequently drove past fields in their cars, honked at girls working in the orchards, and beckoned. Since many girls worked in groups without parental supervision, it was a simple matter for them to slip away. In 1951 a boy known to Fruitlanders as "Little John" loaded his pickup truck with a trader's apples and left with a friend for the carrot fields in Bluewater, some 160 miles away. He induced two girls to accompany him. When they had been gone three days, the girls' parents frantically tried to organize a search party. The mother of Little John and of one girl appeared at the writer's house to ask if he would look for them. But pursuit was not necessary, for the young people appeared at a nearby squaw dance; the boy had sold the apples, but when he returned to Fruitland, he had little money left.

There were also many opportunities for sexual promiscuity near home. With parents away at work it was not difficult for the young to meet. Most boys knew which girls on the Irrigation Project were readily available and watched to see when parents and other relatives left.

Sometimes the boys were caught, and the girls' parents visited the boys' parents to make arrangements for marriage. The boys, however, were not eager, and in six cases, even after the wedding feasts had been prepared, the grooms failed to appear. Little John was not required to marry either girl he had taken to Bluewater. One mother demanded and received $100 from him. Within a few months his own mother arranged a marriage with another girl some ten years older than he, presumably to keep him out of mischief.

While the structure and function of the traditional family and family groups weakened, there was some strengthening of immediate family life. Small families had low status in a community composed until 1950 of extended-family groups. Now they not only made rapid economic strides but also exemplified the kind of family cohesiveness which most Americans consider ideal.

Their orientation toward the white way, somewhat submerged until this time, was now actively pursued and approved. (By comparison, members of large extended-family groupings were subject to more intense pressure to conform, hence adapted more slowly, but—observing those who faced no such pressures —they now resented the restraining force of the traditional family.)

Not only were family conflicts more frequent at Fruitland than in more isolated parts of the reservation; Fruitlanders also had more opportunities for release. They could conveniently leave the reservation for nearby wagework, and they could easily obtain liquor. Probably there were more family conflicts because liquor was rather easily available.[4]

The next chapters will present a series of family case studies revealing the wide range of adjustments which Fruitlanders have made to the changing socioeconomic situation. They will represent different degrees of adjustment and different patterns of satisfactory and unsatisfactory interpersonal relations as well as different psychological responses to the impacts of change. These cases have been chosen to shed some light on the following hypotheses: (1) that situational changes modify traditional patterns of role behavior among members of the family or family groups;[5] (2) that there is a relationship between the size and structure of the family of orientation and adjustment to situational changes;[6] and (3) that adjustment to change situations varies with the clarity with which the family and its membership define the situational changes, their own reference-

---

[4] Drinking, as Kluckhohn states in *Navaho Witchcraft*, p. 54, acts as a "super-ego solvent," after which fights occur.

[5] Talcott Parsons, in "Controlled Institutional Changes," *Essays in Sociological Theory Pure and Applied* (Glencoe, Ill.: Free Press, 1949), p. 318, states that "human behavior may be influenced either through the situation in which people must act, or through 'subjective' elements— their sentiments, goals, attitudes, definition of the situation."

[6] Vogt, *Navaho Veterans*, p. 91.

group norms, and their roles in the rapidly changing scene.[7]

The first series of studies will concern members of Little Ute's extended family—his married sons with their wives and children and a daughter and her husband. These people were at different levels of acculturation and made different kinds of adjustment. Stability characterized those of Little Ute's family who had kept solid roots in Navaho culture—his oldest children (John Jim and Slim Ford's wife) and his fourth son, Harry. Little Ute's second, third, and fifth sons, however, had all been trained in either government or mission boarding schools and behaved in a way indicative of maladjustment whether measured by Navaho or non-Navaho standards. Little Ute's last child was a daughter who in 1950 was about 17; after only two years in the local boarding school, she lived with Little Ute and his wife and made satisfactory adjustment.

The second series of families studied, members of Strong Man's outfit, includes older Navahos faced with the problem of adjustment. The distinguishing characteristic of members of this outfit is that generally the families did not work together (except for one daughter who still worked with an older sister and a younger half-brother). This situation prevailed even though traditionalistic political leadership was long centralized in Strong Man's outfit. Indeed, the very size of this extended family once gave it power; but, particularly after 1950, its position deteriorated. Its leaders had aged, and Strong Man's grandsons disagreed not only among themselves but with their parents. Wage earners who refused to contribute an equal share to family subsistence still expected to share in the food and shelter provided by their father, hence discord was rife.

The third series of studies concerns the various adjustments of newcomers on the Project, some excellent and some badly confused. These newcomers spoke English, acquired non-Nav-

[7] Leonard S. Cottrell, "The Adjustment of the Individual to His Age and Sex Roles," *American Sociological Review*, VII (1942), 618.

aho skills and goods, and adopted values not entirely compatible with the Project's social organization; yet eventually they found their places in the social system in Fruitland. Since, with their skills, they were not dependent on wagework outside the reservation, their primary adjustment was to the Fruitland society into which they had migrated. Those who moved slowly made the most satisfactory adjustments.

CHAPTER X

Long-Time Residents:
Little Ute's Family

LITTLE UTE and his married sons and daughters ceased to function as a family unit after 1950. Before 1950, and especially from 1935 to 1948, Little Ute had largely controlled their undertakings. He sent his sons to help other farmers and in return received help on his farm from other families. But in the last years of the 1940's, Little Ute's sons found working for white men more lucrative.

Little Ute was physically active until a year before his death —from cancer, at age sixty-five, in 1954—and accordingly retained much of his control over the family. Indeed, many Fruitlanders remained vigorous into their seventies, working steadily all their lives but at a leisurely pace; the elders tended to lose their special influence when job priority was given youth.

Born and raised in Sanostee, some fifty miles away, Little Ute married into a Fruitland family in 1905, farmed a few acres on the river bottom in Unit 2 for his mother-in-law, and after twenty years, in exchange for helping dig a larger community canal, obtained a small tract of land for himself. He also worked for three years on the large Project canal, during the 1930's, and as soon as new land was made available, he secured a piece and increased his holding from four to twenty acres. Among the most articulate in protest when "Washingdoon" cut assignments to ten acres, he nevertheless urged his sons and son-in-law to take assignments and increased his and their land holdings whenever he could. He raised five sons and two daughters, all of whom (except for one son who married into a Shiprock family) continued to live in Fruitland. Including his grandchildren, there were twenty-two members of Little Ute's family on the Project in 1954. Considerable friction existed between him and several of his sons and between some of the sons, but very little between Little Ute's wife and the children.

Little Ute drank occasionally when he had access to bootleg wine. At such times, usually once every two or three months, he saddled up his horse and rode around the unit, greeting passers-by and families cordially. At meetings when he was sober he was always called upon to make a speech. The people listened intently but whispered among themselves, "Too bad that he drinks so much."

Because he spoke eloquently against stock reduction and other government programs, he was for a time prominent in community politics. But after he was elected chapter president in 1943, his influence diminished rapidly, largely because of his drinking. In any event he did not really want a political position, for he held a kinship status which placed him in a unique role as consultant. During the late 1940's and early 1950's he was frequently consulted by his brother-in-law, who was the local delegate to the Tribal Council, and by his brother, who represented the neighboring District. Little Ute enjoyed his informal position and the "inside" (though often distorted) information that it gave him. One of his sons remarked, "When my father goes to the store [two miles away] it takes him all day. He talks with everybody that he meets."

Little Ute and his wife lived together for over forty-five years without major difficulties. She seems to have tolerated her husband's drinking, for in seven years of field work the writer heard not one word of gossip about any quarrel between them. Little Ute was an extremely hard worker. When not working in the fields, he mended fences. As soon as he harvested his last crop, he left for work in the carrot fields at Phoenix or Bluewater. With the money earned there he purchased silver and made ornaments for sale at squaw dances, rodeos, and fairs. When no work was to be done at his farm or his hogan or on his sons' farms, he worked for the trader as a sheepherder.

Little Ute's wife kept busy herding sheep while at the same time caring for her children and later her grandchildren, some of whom were her constant companions. In 1950 she felt isolated from the rest of the family because she spent much of her time at a sheep camp two miles south of the Project and because her grandchildren were growing up and leaving for school. (One reason for this interest in education was that the parents wanted more healthful living conditions for their children than could be had in their grandmother's home.) At the death of her husband, she went to live with her youngest daughter and the daughter's husband.

Four households in Little Ute's extended family will be treated in some detail: those of John Jim, Slim Ford, Junior Begay, and Jerry Begay. Two sons and one daughter, Luke, Harry, and Joan, are first briefly described.

The third son, Luke, farmed in Fruitland for a year before leaving, in part because he constantly quarreled with his brothers and with his father. As a child he had had numerous sings performed over him and was therefore familiar with chants as well as with the Navaho world view. He later attended the Shiprock boarding school and worked for non-Navahos. He imposed upon his relatives, as Navahos often do, but never reciprocated; others in the family constantly commented upon this.

The fourth son, Harry, left for school soon after this study began. Although his rearing at home was much like Junior's, Jerry's, and Luke's, unlike them he had received no formal education until he was eighteen years of age. He was thus well rooted in the Navaho way of life when he elected to participate in the special five-year training program for older Navaho children. He seemed to sense that he needed some knowledge of English and some vocational training. He felt that the limited land base on the Project prevented him from obtaining his own farm. He learned English and office methods sufficiently well during his first year of formal education to get a clerical job at the Phoenix school, and after two years of school work he had a permanent job. He married a girl whom he met at Phoenix, left her with his family while he was in the Marine Corps, came home in 1953 when he heard his father was ill, and worked his father's farm (but did not take over the assignment). His wife, in the meantime, worked in a restaurant across the river. After Little Ute's death, Harry became boys' adviser at the Shiprock school, returning occasionally to visit his mother.

Little Ute and his wife arranged a marriage for their youngest child, Joan, when she was sixteen. Sam David was twice Joan's age. On the day set for their wedding he was intent on running away, but their life together has nevertheless been happy. They lived in a tent beside her mother's log cabin (Sam did not practice mother-in-law avoidance as did the older brother-in-law, Susie Ford's husband). He always managed to get jobs, for he had learned fluent English at the Methodist mission school.[1] He worked for several years at the local trading post, as a boys' adviser at the Fruitland boarding school, as a laborer for the gas company, as a tractor driver for the government, and finally as a clerk in an army surplus store in town. The Fruitland dele-

[1] The school expelled Sam for smoking—ironically enough, for he never again smoked. Although he served three years in the Navy, he did not learn to drink. His strong objection to drinking indeed sometimes caused friction between him and his father-in-law; Joan reprimanded her father often for attempting to force Sam to join him in drinking.

gates asked him to become a tribal policeman, but he refused because of the social ostracism which he felt that he would have to face.

Although Sam's weekly income was a fairly steady $50, he could never save, but he helped his in-laws whenever they held sings or wanted money for car repairs, wine, or medical payments. At the same time he made car payments regularly, clothed and fed himself and his growing family well, and took his children to the doctors in town regularly. He realized that as long as he lived with his father-in-law he would remain in debt but felt that he had no other recourse; his wife would not leave her parents to establish an independent household unit. At Little Ute's death, Sam applied for and received one of his assignments. His mother-in-law continued to live with him and his wife, but there appeared to be little strain in the household, partly, perhaps, because he worked in town throughout the week.

John Jim, Little Ute's oldest son, was about forty-five in 1950. He and his wife had made a satisfactory adjustment to each changing situation through a series of compromises. He spoke no English but had a personality that non-Navahos liked, and he was able to find positions in some of which he learned much about the non-Navaho world.

He had had tuberculosis since childhood, but through proper rest and care, under advisement of medicine men, he kept the disease arrested most of the time; and when the condition became active, as in 1952, he brought his "sick-all-over feeling" quickly under control, he relates, by undergoing ceremonials and by restricting his physical activities. He had participated in sings and been sung over when very young, and he remained a firm believer in the Navaho way of life. In addition, he was treated for various sicknesses in the mission hospital.

Until he could obtain his own farm, John Jim lived with his parents, herding their sheep and helping on their farm. Because

Little Ute found him a good worker, he did not allow him to go to school. By the time the government made farm assignments available, John Jim was married. He worked with his father on the canal and eventually took an assignment in Unit 1, near his wife's parents' farm. A second assignment obtained later, closer to Unit 2, was not productive because of the high alkali content in the soil, but he continued to live there because he could visit his parents with considerably less loss of time; later he could commute easily to work at the trading post.

Several times John Jim left to work off-reservation, but he always found home more satisfactory. Even living in Unit 1 had caused him some uneasiness. Whenever his father or his brothers needed an extra hand to help erect a hogan or to help plow a field because the season was advancing, he would appear on Sundays to contribute his share of work. When he could not come himself, he lent his team, wagon, or implements to his relatives without hesitation.

By 1950 John Jim's farm was one of the most productive in Unit 1, and his health was reasonably good. He was, however, dissatisfied with his job at the trading post. The gas company rejected his job application (because x-rays revealed scar tissue on his lungs), but he soon found a position as a laborer for a paving contractor in Farmington. A year of heavy work affected his health. Little Ute sponsored a sing for him, and after about six months of rest he returned to work at the trading post.

John Jim's one child died soon after birth, and he and his wife thereafter transferred their affections to his nieces and nephews. He felt especially close to his own brothers and to his parents and did them favors or gave them what silverwork he had time to manufacture. His younger brothers all looked to him for advice and for intercession when they were in trouble. Sometimes they asked him for advice on such technical matters as repair of a carburetor or a walking plow; although he had had no formal education, he had acquired considerable skill in handling tools. When he could not repair an article himself, he told his brothers and his father where they should take the equipment —knowledge he had gained while working for the trader. John's brothers also found him a fun-loving companion, always ready for a good time. They went hunting on horseback for rabbits and prairie dogs before they had cars. Later they took frequent trips to Durango and Cortez, Colorado, and to Shiprock.[2]

Little Ute's second child, Slim Ford's wife, was some forty years old in 1950. She and Slim, like her brother John Jim, were Navaho-oriented and secure, yet able to adapt themselves to the changing world. Her parents and Slim's had arranged their marriage around 1930; neither had gone to school, and they spoke no English. Before the large Project canal was opened, the couple lived with Little Ute and the rest of his family. When assignments became available, he moved to his own farm, about half a mile away, and built a stone house for his wife and children. He was a good son-in-law—quiet, hardworking, obedient. He participated in all sings given by the family and practiced mother-in-law avoidance. He and his wife made no effort to see non-Navahos except for economic purposes.

Although Slim and his wife had been raised in the traditional manner, both had younger brothers who were educated,[3] and they wanted their own children to know about the white way. Their five children were enrolled in school as soon as they were old enough: the oldest boy in the mission school, where he

[2] It may be observed that John Jim saw little of his wife or her family, since, except for returning home at night and working his fields weekends, he seemed to spend most of his time either at the store or with his own brothers. Except for one sing held for him at his own hogan, his sings were always carried on at his mother's.

[3] All three of Slim's younger brothers had a real command of English, and one went through college (and never returned home).

completed high school with honors in 1950, and the others first in the local day school and then in different off-reservation Indian Service and public schools. (One daughter stayed at home to help care for the younger children until she was old enough to participate in the special program of the Intermountain Indian School at Brigham City, Utah.) Raised in a happy atmosphere at home, among uncles and aunts and grandparents, these children adjusted to their schools without the running-away adventures of many Fruitland children.

The parents demonstrated their capacity to adjust in other ways. Their house, built before World War II, was a rectangular building of stone, equipped with commercial windows and door. By 1949 they owned two beds, a number of tables and benches, and a combination cooking and heating stove. Adding an English name to their descriptive Navaho name, they began to identify themselves by given names and this new family surname. Thus, instead of calling himself by his descriptive name, Slim Policeman's Grandson, Slim was Slim Ford. Similarly his wife began to be known as Lucy Ford, and the older children as Jim, Nelson, and Nancy Ford—in part through the influence of Mrs. Ford's younger brother Junior Begay but largely, no doubt, because of ideas the children brought home. Young Jim was especially sensitive about Navaho living conditions, indicated that he preferred the white man's way of life, and until he was graduated from high school never attended a ceremonial.

Before 1950, the children led a busy life, the older taking care of the younger, hitching up the team and guiding it skillfully behind the cultivator, hoeing industriously. Although their father and, later, the older boys were away working during the growing season, the fields were kept in good order. They enjoyed wagon rides to the trading post for water (and candy and pop) or to their grandparents for long visits or a meal of mutton. Father's return was a happy occasion, for he brought new clothing, toys, and cash.

In 1950, after his graduation from high school, Jim, the

oldest boy, went to college. He financed his first term by a tribal loan and summer wages, his second by assistance from his father and brother. Following a year at college he went to work.

Working sixty hours a week, Slim and Nelson, his second son, now earned about $600 a month. Steady workers, they held their jobs long after many others quit or were discharged. In early 1952 Jim was drafted for military service, and a short while later Nelson was called (he soon married). Once again the family's sole support, Slim Ford increased his work week to seven days to augment his overtime pay, keeping up the exhausting pace for months at a time without rest. Twice he took time to drive to Jemez Pueblo for curing ceremonies; though he was not ill, he complained of stiffness in the joints, probably caused by constant exposure to the cold winds.

Slim's expenditures during the period of high wages were large, especially on cars and trucks. In late 1950 he paid $1,600 for a 1949 Dodge sedan which had gone 20,000 miles according to the speedometer but at least twice that far if one judged by its condition. The steering mechanism and the springs were in such poor condition that the car was unsafe; repairs cost Slim Ford over $100 within a month. After he had paid $825 on the sedan, he turned it in on a new pickup truck. A year later, when he had almost completed payments on the new truck, he replaced it with a larger model. Six months later, deciding that this new truck was too large, he again traded for a new, smaller model.

In 1953 the Slim Fords had living with them their daughter Nancy and her husband, Nelson's wife,[4] and the smaller children, though during the school year two children were away.

---

[4] Contrary to Navaho custom, Nelson and Nancy had found their own marriage mates. When Nancy, living with a boy who worked in town, wanted to get married, the boy did not know what his clan was, and Slim and Lucy Ford withheld the Navaho ceremony until they received a letter which, indicating his clan membership, assured them that there would be no incest (through clan membership) in the union. The marriage broke up within five months, after the husband had left for wagework.

Jim and Nelson were still in the armed forces. During Nelson's absence his wife worked in town; upon his return the couple established residence with his parents.

The final adjustment of the educated children of this family was still uncertain. So far the behavior of the older children had been much like that of most American middle-class adolescents; they had participated in school athletics, achieved good scholastic averages, and worn clothes like those of their classmates. At the same time they had been good children when measured by Navaho standards. When not at school, all, even the youngest, helped with chores and farm work. All but Jim participated in Navaho sings and squaw dances. Undoubtedly their adjustment will depend largely upon the circumstances of their long-time encounters in the competitive non-Navaho world.

Little Ute's second son was Junior Begay, about thirty-six years old in 1954, married for about seven years, and with one son. Junior had had non-Navaho companions as a boy and again during the war; his deep-rooted dilemma was inability to decide between Navaho and non-Navaho values.

Junior's marriage in 1946 was not arranged by his parents, like his older brother's and his sister's. He had not courted for long the girl he married, though they had attended the same boarding school and he had often watched her play basketball. She too showed a preference for some white values, generally the superficial ones.

Junior herded sheep until he was about eight years old, then enrolled in the Shiprock boarding school. He stayed at Shiprock for six years, returning for summer vacations and sometimes walking the eighteen miles home on weekends, when he was homesick or when he wanted to eat mutton. From his account he enjoyed school in spite of the rigid routine, but he was also glad to leave when the time came.

Junior's dilemma apparently can be traced to influences immediately after boarding school. He had non-Navaho friends, played well with them, and found himself valuing their way of life more than that of the Navaho. He refused to have sings performed over him. Junior continued to herd sheep but began to spend more time working across the river. He obtained a job as a farm hand and, later, as a laborer in a brickyard. During this time he became acquainted with a family of white boys. He spent much time with them and soon found himself with few Navaho friends of his own age.

In 1938 Junior received an assignment, even though he was not yet married and according to land-assignment policy only married couples could receive assignments. (The Agency apparently made the assignment in an effort to appease his father, then as always an outspoken critic of government policy, and his mother's half-brother, one of the leaders in Fruitland.) During the next several years Junior attempted to farm, but not very industriously; he found that his soil was waterlogged and tended toward alkalinity. Although the irrigation engineer and his crew dug a drainage ditch part way through the field, the soil did not become properly productive for several years.

When war was declared, Junior was drafted. He took his basic training at Fort Sill, Oklahoma, and in southern California, was shipped to England, received shrapnel wounds in Normandy which disabled his shoulder, and returned and spent the rest of the war at a hospital in Santa Fe.

During this period, in spite of his incapacity and hospitalization, he was happy. He had been the only Indian in his unit and had mixed socially with white boys, who, he said, liked to have him around and delighted in calling him "Chief." He also enjoyed Santa Fe and convalescence there with non-Navaho friends. As an ambulatory patient he could visit in Santa Fe and Albuquerque.

When Junior was discharged in 1946, he returned to Fruitland. For several years he received no disability pension. "What is being done for the veterans?" his father wanted to know and meanwhile did all of Junior's farm work. Junior had no funds to buy farm implements or horses, and he was unable to use his disabled shoulder. He was in a state of mental depression.

In 1949 he began to receive pension checks regularly, which enabled him to purchase items he needed to begin farming. By 1950 he owned a wagon, a sit-down plow and cultivator, a hay rake, and a mowing machine. He also purchased a team of horses in La Plata, Colorado.

The war years presumably satisfied Junior's need for white companionship, for although he talked at great length about his "war buddies" (without mentioning anything about his experiences with them), he now never visited non-Navahos except on business or when he had been drinking. Otherwise he was sullen whenever he dealt with white people. He was concerned about his disability, which prevented his working for wages. What regular income he had, his disability compensation, he shared freely with his friends and relatives. He held Christmas and birthday parties, too, and gave presents generously.

Junior's main interest was in his home. He rarely visited his parents or his brothers for social purposes. And unlike his sister and his brothers, he did not send his only child to his parents whenever he wanted a "baby sitter." He either stayed at home or sent the child to his older sister. Junior's wife also seldom left the home. About three times she visited her parents. After Junior bought a truck, her visits were more frequent. She was very quiet. She spoke English but was not responsive to white persons. She often took her son to bathe at the school showers, and she constantly admonished him for putting his fingers or any foreign matter into his mouth. Besides seeing that her child and her husband were always dressed in clean and freshly pressed clothes, she herself consistently dressed like a white woman.

In 1949, after considerable pressure from his father, Junior had a squaw dance performed for him. Until this time he had resisted, partly because he did not feel it would help him but partly because he brooded over what his "white buddies" might think of him, in spite of the fact that he had neither seen nor heard from them. When the writer visited Junior, he talked repeatedly about his "buddies" and asked what white people thought about Navaho sings. Perhaps as a result of airing such conflicts with the writer and other fieldworkers and seeing them at ceremonials, he at last consented to participate in one of his own.

During the same period he made noticeable improvements on his house, hiring non-Navaho help to put on a new asphalt shingled roof, to build a division wall between bedroom and kitchen, and to remodel the brick chimney to accommodate the exhaust from the heating stove in the bedroom and the new cook stove in the kitchen. Besides a bed, a table, and chairs, he purchased from a mail-order house a pantry and a portable closet and installed them in his home. Occasionally he helped his father and his brothers and sisters in their farm work, lending them his sit-down cultivator and mowing machine. When they helped him in return for use of his implements, he paid them in kind or in cash.

When, in 1950, Slim Ford, Junior's own younger brother Jerry Begay, and others in the unit began to get jobs with the gas company, their income surpassed his own $180 per month. Still, when he rode into town with clan relatives in his own age group, it was he who had credit at the store and could always borrow money to pay for the gas. Under pressure from friends and relatives, he spent more and more money on these trips. For a time, when his wife worked at the school, he stayed home to care for his four-year-old son. Later, when he was absent for long weekends, he sent the children to Lucy Ford's.

In 1952 Junior was able to buy a car with help from the

Veterans' Administration. He had been brooding about his disability, and acquisition of a vehicle seemed to raise his morale. The car changed his work and recreational habits. Within a period of eight months he traveled over 32,000 miles. He serviced the pickup regularly but had bad luck with tires, breaking and replacing three at a cost of $50 each. Although at first he did not mix drinking with driving, he could not continue to resist his friends' invitation to go to town and to Colorado for liquor. As a result he had several accidents which required extensive repairs; fortunately, he was never critically injured.

Jerry Begay, though reared in a family still fairly well integrated, suffered experiences in school and humiliation among non-Navaho fellow workers which explained, at least in part, his inability to control his desires.

Until 1950 Jerry led a life like that of many other Navaho boys of his age. He was close to his family, spent six years away from home to attend school, and was too young to be drafted into the army. Growing up in a time of much turmoil between the Navahos and the government, he watched his neighbors becoming poorer and poorer. He was a child when the stock-reduction program was fought through, but talks with his father and other older people in the long winter evenings made these experiences a part of him.

Jerry was the fifth child born to Little Ute and his wife. Although the school that he attended was only fifteen miles away, it seemed farther to the boy; in those days Navahos rode to town on horseback or on wagons, and a one-way ride usually took three to four hours. In school the young Indian children were told to forget about those "superstitious" ways with which they were familiar. Jerry objected, for he had learned much about the Navaho world view, taboos, and the general rules of behavior which ordered his life at home and kept him from being punished by supernatural forces.

Before Jerry finally resolved to quit school, he learned to

read, to write, and speak English well. He enjoyed learning, for his skills gave him an opportunity to satisfy his curiosity. He read newspapers and magazines even though he did not always understand them. Indeed, he continued reading and writing even after he left school; by the time he was fourteen he had a fair comprehension of what he read.

When Jerry returned home from school, he herded sheep for his father and mother. He also learned to plow, to irrigate the fields, and to sing Navaho songs. He liked to sit around the camp fires and gossip about what went on in the community and in the world outside the reservation. The news that he had gleaned from newspapers, though perhaps weeks or months old, he reported to others in his family. He was proud that he could dispense the news, and what he learned seemed to him the more significant because he also knew about Navaho folklore and behaved like a Navaho who "had many relatives." But his application of what he read brought him misfortune, for his comprehension of complex phenomena as explained in the papers was immature. After he read about the "sit-down strikes" held to obtain wage raises in industry, he attempted to organize one among the Indians who worked in an apple orchard across the river. When the farmer came to see why the apples were not being picked, Jerry told him that he and the others were on strike for higher pay. The farmer told the fruit pickers, Navaho men and women, that Jerry was a "smart aleck" and a trouble-maker and ordered Jerry, as well as any others who wished to continue the strike, to leave. The papers that Jerry read had contained nothing about the possibility of such humiliations.

In 1947 Little Ute arranged with another family of old residents that Jerry marry their daughter. Many friends and relatives were invited to attend the Navaho wedding. When the ceremony was over, Jerry and his wife remained at the sheep camp of the wife's family, but within a week Jerry was back at his own parents' home. Thereafter, the couple lived for short and long periods of time at three places: his mother-in-law's sheep camp some sixteen miles south, his father-in-law's assignment on the extreme eastern end of the Project, and his own parents' hogan in Unit 2. In 1949, after an older brother decided to give up farming, Jerry's father helped him buy the improvements on the farm and to take over the assignment; Jerry then had a fourth place to live.

By 1950, three years after his marriage, Jerry had left the reservation twice to work on the railroads. While he was away, his wife stayed with her mother and his oldest child with his parents. On both occasions he was accompanied by his father-in-law to Colorado, Wyoming, and Utah. He saw many things that he had read about during his younger days. Nevertheless he felt insecure in the white society, and he followed the behavioral pattern set by older Navahos.

As a boy he had seen the uncertainties that developed in others as a result of town contacts, especially Gallup. He was fascinated by the stories he had heard about the "wild life," but at the same time he refused to go there himself and he would not drink. However, his friends pressured him into drinking and indulging in other deviant forms of behavior, and his attitudes changed. Indeed, he went to the opposite extreme within a very few months after his first stable job.

When the gas company began recruiting laborers at Fruitland, Jerry was one of the first to get a job. The company quickly promoted him from one position to another because he was able to follow instructions and because he himself was not satisfied with work which involved only the use of a shovel. Thus, within a month he held a job as a "jack" or air-hammer operator, which paid $1.55 an hour.

The semiskilled position gave him renewed confidence, and he seemed to want to prove his maturity by doing things that he had formerly avoided. He wished to "belong." Therefore, when older men urged him to drink wine with them, he did. He had one major automobile accident, which resulted in the loss of his job, and three others which sent him to the hospital.

Jerry's family life was at first relatively happy because there were many relatives to visit and because his family's needs were not great. As children came, one or the other of the boys was left with grandparents. When Jerry and his father-in-law worked for the gas company, both purchased trucks and could now easily visit each other and other relatives. Even after Jerry wrecked his truck and had his driver's license revoked, he drove his father-in-law's vehicle, being careful to avoid state highways.

The accidents which incapacitated Jerry made him and his wife and children more dependent upon relatives. The state police investigating his first accident, north of Gallup on Highway 666, charged him with drunken driving. Jerry's father made several trips to the sheriff's office in Gallup, some 120 miles away, to settle the case out of court. During the six months that Jerry spent at the hospital his father visited him three times. Moreover, Little Ute worked Jerry's farm with his brother Junior's help. After deducting their share, they gave Jerry the remainder of the income from the sale of farm products.

For four months after Jerry's discharge from the hospital, he remained near the Project. His father hired a singer, and a ceremony was held. Only a few relatives attended, for almost all able-bodied males were at work and the women had no means of transportation. After the sing Jerry and his family moved back to his own farm and lived there through most of 1952, going to his wife's sheep camp occasionally to look after his wife's herd.

In early 1953 Jerry again secured a job with the gas company. After working for several months, he was again discharged. In the next six months he held three different jobs, as car washer, small-tractor driver for the government, and finally truck driver's helper for a transfer company.

Of all the positions which Jerry had held, that with the transfer company had the most promise of permanency. It gave him more satisfaction, too, than did the other positions, for it enabled him to drive and also to visit the stores after he unloaded the merchandise. He seemed to have settled down. He commuted from his farm to Farmington daily and returned home with groceries that he had purchased in town.

Jerry's young wife was perhaps more fortunate than other wives of her age, but at the same time she suffered from many problems created by her husband. She was fortunate that her parents had a farm and also a sheep camp nearby. Whenever Jerry was away from home for long periods working or in the hospital or convalescing at his mother's home, she returned to her mother's hogan. Unlike some other families, her parents owned several hundred head of sheep, and she herself had thirty; when she returned to their home her presence was not an imposition. At sheep camp, too, she had the company of her younger unmarried sister who herded in the absence of the parents.

When Jerry stayed with his family during his convalescence, she rarely visited her husband. Only after he was able to use crutches and return to his own hogan did she consent to join him. In this manner she avoided conflict with her mother-in-law. Meanwhile she learned to drive her father's car and could visit her own family whenever Jerry left for work. If he failed to return from work, she went to her own family's hogan.

CHAPTER XI

Long-Time Residents: Strong Man's Outfit

IN 1955 Strong Man and nine other members of his outfit (six adults of the next generation and three of the third) had assignments in Unit 2. One other family member had an assignment in Unit 3, and two were in the livestock business. Since most of the biological families which comprised Strong Man's outfit were as large as Little Ute's, some will be by-passed in order to describe others in detail.

With so many brothers and sisters, living in a circumscribed area and holding among them one-third of the total number of assignments in Unit 2, this group had once been a potent political force. But within a fifteen-year period they became the most poorly organized outfit in the unit. Sickness, witchcraft fears and accusations, and personality disorganization had a deleterious effect from 1940, but it was not until the prosperity of the early 1950's that group functioning broke down completely. Individually, some fared badly in the period of adjustment, some satisfactorily, and some were unchanged. However, the outfit as a whole seemed increasingly maladjusted.

Indeed, the families of Little Ute and Strong Man, long the very closest knit of traditionalist Unit 2, have shown more signs of stress and dissension than any others in Fruitland. Under their traditional way of life Navahos were forced to neutralize hostility because they had to call upon others, particularly their close relatives, in order to eke out their subsistence. In attempting to enforce this collateral pattern when it was no longer functional, family members created additional tensions. In the changing situation they found themselves at odds with one another because of conflicting orientations. Young men and women in these extended families, particularly those who had had formal education, were unable to reconcile old patterns with the changed situation. The uneducated younger members realized that something was wrong but did not know what.[1]

Four persons, Atcitty Jim's wife, Charley Bidoni, Salow's brother-in-law, and Johnson Jones, were Strong Man's first wife's children by her previous marriage. All of these but Charley Bidoni lived on the Irrigation Project (Salow's brother-in-law did not live in Unit 2). Strong Man's children by his first wife, Ray Johnson, Kee Warner, Hosteen Benally's wife, and Allan William's widow, and their families lived in Unit 2. Johnson Jones, Ray Johnson, and Kee Warner were married to sisters. Strong Man had three children by his second wife, all of whom lived with the Hosteen Benallys (who had no children of their own), and four by his third.

Strong Man himself, the old man of this outfit, was in 1955 still active physically at the age of seventy-five, though he had generally retired from community life some twenty years before, presumably because of poor eyesight and hearing. He still functioned as a singer when called upon. Furthermore, as

[1] Vogt, in his *Navaho Veterans*, p. 91, found that "large extended family groupings tend to function as repositories of conservative Navaho patterns and values, to exercise a negative influence on rapid acculturation in that the individual members of these families undergo a more thorough orientation to Navaho culture."

his third wife he had married a girl one-third his age and fathered four children.

Strong Man lived in a log cabin that he had built thirty to forty years ago. Its design indicated his early contact with non-Navahos. He was well known in the valley at the turn of the century for his riding skill. Apparently he was never a forceful man and for this reason never considered becoming a headman. He worked for non-Navahos and tilled his small farm.

He forbade his own and his first wife's children to attend school. Kee Warner alone ran away to school, but after some years his parents tied him to the reservation by marrying him to a woman who spoke no English.

As the children obtained separate assignments, they tended to become immersed in their own work and called on Strong Man only when they wanted a sing performed. (Among his children and numerous grandchildren, only one became a singer.) Strong Man worked his ten acres with the help of young sons by his second wife. His third wife, extremely unacculturated and almost deaf, helped with the field work when not caring for her own four children. Besides his small income from the farm Strong Man received welfare benefits—old-age assistance and aid to dependent children. In addition, he occasionally received a small check from oil leases on land in the off-reservation checkerboard area.[2] Because he had long ago restricted his social activities on account of his physical impairments, he lived aloof from change, except for his interest in welfare payments and oil leases.

Atcitty Jim, born near Fruitland in the early 1880's, moved to the grassland just south of the irrigated valley when he married a daughter of Strong Man's first wife. As farm land

[2] The land immediately to the east of the reservation is called "checkerboard." It was created during the late 1880's when the Santa Fe Railroad was given all odd-numbered sections in the square miles on each side of the right of way.

became available in Unit 2, Atcitty and his oldest son took
neighboring assignments. In 1950 he and his sons held about
thirty-three acres.

Fruitland's social and psychological pressures were highly
exaggerated in Atcitty's family. In no other family had parents
and all the sons, daughters, sons-in-law, daughters-in-law, and
grandchildren been as closely united. During the 1940's four
married sons, their wives and children, a daughter, and her
husband and three children still lived periodically with Atcitty
and his wife. When at home the family members occupied two
stone houses, one frame house, and several tents. In addition, the
family owned a modern stone hogan, the largest of its kind in
the valley, located at the sheep camp of Atcitty's wife about
a mile south of the farm. The excellence and the number of
houses in the family, indicative of wealth by Fruitland standards, were due largely to the skill of the second son, Frank,
trained as a stone mason and carpenter in Indian Bureau schools.

Atcitty's early youth was spent on the reservation except for
brief periods at two federal schools. He said that, although he
wanted to continue his education, poor health and trachoma
forced him to leave. But even his little off-reservation experience
helped him get jobs with the land-survey crew which extended
the boundaries of the reservation during the early 1900's.
During this period and again much later, when most Navahos
relied on traders for credit and for banking services, he deposited money in commercial banks.

Although Atcitty's early associations with non-Navahos were
instructive and enabled him to move about freely and con-
fidently in their world, when on the reservation he remained
thoroughly Navaho in his beliefs about man's relations with
man, with nature, and with the supernatural. The illnesses which
forced him to leave school were "cured" by sings performed by
Navaho medicine men. This was after school authorities had

told him that he would become blind and chronically ill with tuberculosis.

Atcitty's wife did not speak English, nor did any of her brothers and sisters. On principle and perhaps because she wanted her children's help at home and at sheep camp, she opposed their going to school, and Atcitty did not force the issue. Of his seven living children, only two attended school.

Yet Atcitty's own command of English, almost unique among older men at the time of the stock-reduction program, enabled him to act as spokesman and council delegate for Unit 2. As The People's representative he was vigorous in his protests against government programs.

Around 1940 the three children of Atcitty's daughter died of tuberculosis; her husband accused Atcitty's brother of bewitching the children, shot the "witch," and then shot himself.

In the early war years, Atcitty took three of his sons to Nevada, where they worked in a mine. Atcitty's knowledge of English enabled him to secure a job as foreman of the Navaho work crew. He collected his sons' wages, gave them a few dollars for spending money, mailed a small amount to his wife, and deposited the remainder in the bank. By the time they returned to Fruitland, they had over $1,600 in the bank under Atcitty Jim's name. When his sons asked for some of the money that they had earned, in order to buy agricultural implements, Atcitty refused.

In 1946 the wife of Atcitty's second son, Frank, died of tuberculosis. Frank then left home and worked on the railroad until 1950, returning home only periodically. The other boys also left for work. The oldest, Atcitty Begay, returned in spring and summer to help on the farm, since part of it was assigned to him.

During the late 1940's Atcitty Jim and his wife had only one daughter-in-law at home, Begay's wife, Alice—and there was constant conflict between her and her mother-in-law, especially over health, education, and diet. Alice had had a formal education at the mission school and could not adjust herself adequately to Navaho life. Despite gossip and ridicule whenever she tried to practice modern homemaking, nevertheless she attempted to emulate white practices for the welfare of her seven children. She did not, for example, allow her children to spoon food from a common bowl, particularly when eating with her sister-in-law, who had active tuberculosis. Atcitty's wife could not understand why Alice was so intent on owning plates and washing them in soapy water. Alice wished to send her children to school; her mother-in-law wanted them to tend her sheep. Alice believed that she and her family should move away, but her husband chose to remain. She believed that Begay lacked the courage to support her views. At last, when Begay obtained work with the gas company, east of Farmington, Alice could legitimately encourage her husband to rent a house in town. She too took a job.

Frank, after being absent from home almost continuously from the time of his first wife's death, remarried in 1950 and brought his new wife home, where he remained thereafter. This wife pleased Frank's mother, but, facing the same pressures as Alice, she persuaded Frank to erect a tent by the river, about a quarter of a mile from the farm where he worked.

Ned, another son, also brought home a young and educated wife, whom he had met while she was working in a café in town. Because life on the farm seemed dull to her, she returned to Farmington and took a job as a waitress. Soon she and Ned parted because of differences in interest.

Nelson Jim, the youngest son, married a girl from Unit 2 in 1947 when he returned from the armed forces. He moved in with his wife's family and because of the shortage of assignments in Unit 2 had to help his father-in-law and take whatever jobs were available. After 1950, under the impact of prosperity, his family and that of his father-in-law seemed to become completely disorganized. Promiscuity, brawls, and episodes of wife beating were prevalent. Yet both the older and the younger couples remained together. In 1954 Nelson Jim became a member of the tribal police force.

Between 1950 and 1952 each of Atcitty's four sons purchased motor vehicles more expensive than they could afford, though they held jobs. Whenever they could not meet the payments, Atcitty drew from his bank account; and whenever they needed tires or money for repairs, they again asked Atcitty for their "share" of the savings. Within two years the bank account was almost gone, and Atcitty could not look forward to the pleasure of drawing interest. With easy mobility, the boys no longer stayed at home even when they were not working. Although Atcitty attempted to unite the family, the boys did not respond; not one of them assumed any leadership.

After 1946, too, when Atcitty's age began to prevent him from working vigorously, his status in the community declined. According to current gossip, Atcitty talked a good deal about farming and livestock methods but neither he nor his sons engaged in these practices. By 1952 Atcitty spent all of his time herding sheep, a task which required only that he ride his horse; his wife felt that he contributed more in this way than he could on the farm. As the community became more and more preoccupied with wagework and with non-Navaho ways, his position as leader fell further. His adherence to old beliefs was a subject for ridicule, and he was considered too old to guide because he no longer worked as did others even in his age group. Atcitty could only look back at his sheaf of correspondence from government agents in Washington, Santa Fe, and Window Rock as evidence that he was once a leader.

With all his able-bodied sons engaged in wagework, his

wife and grandchildren took over the care of the farm; predictably, the yield was small,[3] as was that from livestock in those years of unusually light rainfall. At marketing time the lambs averaged less than forty pounds each.

With such a reduction in income, Atcitty looked elsewhere for cash which he could contribute to his wife. Whenever he was able to free himself from herding, he sought information about welfare aid. With the help of a student fieldworker, he wrote letters to the Federal Security Office in San Francisco, stating that regular social security deductions had been taken from his pay checks in Nevada and that he was eager to get the benefits. Soon he received a check for $200.70, representing benefits for the months between December, 1950, and August, 1951, and thereafter he received a monthly check for $22.30. The regular payments met Atcitty's needs but not those of his grandchildren. He therefore requested and received state aid for dependent children by indicating in the application form that the children's parents had deserted them.

By 1952 Atcitty's family was a bare shell of the functioning unit that it once was. The only persons who remained continuously on the farm and at the sheep camp were Atcitty, his wife, a daughter, and his grandchildren when they were not in school. Nevertheless the high cost of feeding the grandchildren with little help from their parents was a heavy drain on the family's resources. The whole situation was psychologically most painful to Atcitty; he could not depend on his sons at all. He had always taken much pleasure in traveling whenever he had the opportunity, but now he could not rely on his sons to take him; they always seemed to have other

[3] The crop value for the combined farms of Jim and his wife dropped from about $2,000 in 1949 to less than $1,500 in 1952, according to Fruitland Irrigation Project Crop Reports; the estimates, made by government agents, are probably too high, for much of the field was either in alfalfa which should have been plowed under several years earlier or not planted at all because the land was waterlogged.

plans. Perhaps in this way they struck back at him, for although their share of what he had saved for them in Nevada enabled them to make payments on their cars, he had refused earlier to help them buy agricultural implements. It was particularly painful for Atcitty to draw the last of his savings to pay for his sons' drinking fines.

Still Atcitty did not sit idly by, watching his family disintegrate. He tried to get the boys to give their checks to him so that he could invest some of their money in farm implements, but they refused. He then divided his assignment (without formal transfer) among his three sons who did not have farms in hope of bringing them back; he could not persuade them to return, however, or even to begin contributing more than a few dollars toward the purchase of clothing for their own children. The first son and his wife, Begay and Alice, were by now completely demoralized; the second son, Frank, away from his father's home since 1943 except for brief periods, appeared to have settled down on the white man's side of the river; the remainder of the family were engaged in wagework but neither saved their money nor purchased wisely. The daughter, who remarried after the death of her first husband, was ill with tuberculosis. Her present husband worked on the railroad most of each year but often requested that cash be sent him to help pay fines.

Ray Johnson was Strong Man's own first child. He was apparently rebellious in his youth, particularly over the fact that Strong Man did not let him go to school. Ray was made to herd sheep while a younger brother, Kee Warner, went to the Shiprock boarding school and later to the Haskell Institute at Lawrence, Kansas. When his own boys, Bob and Pete, became of age, he sent them to the school at Shiprock for six years, but he kept his daughter at home to herd sheep. During the early days of the Project, Ray remained politically in the background; Atcitty Jim was the spokesman for the outfit. Ray waited until after the war to take active part in community affairs and was then elected chapter president.

He called the meetings and presided. He was a striking figure, with his maroon shirt, tall black felt hat, dark glasses, and heavy silver belt. He spoke in a monotone but with sufficient inflection to hold the people's attention. He was proud of his leadership and proud that, as leader, he abstained from alcohol.

By 1950 Ray became involved in family difficulties. On their return from the war and Air Force service in Germany, his two sons were unable to adjust to an orderly civilian life. In the summer and fall of 1950, Ray and his son Bob were hired by the gas company. When Bob was fired the next year, Ray was the main provider for the family. Bob was to be responsible for the fields, but except for periodic mowing of hay on his father's farm he did very little; Ray's wife and daughter undertook the farm work. Ray was held partly to blame for the indolence and violence of both his sons.

During the industrialization period Ray attempted to hold the community together by regular meetings, but few persons attended; he himself became so discouraged that at length he stopped calling them. The 1951 elections revealed general dissatisfaction with his leadership. He finished third in the race for the presidency. As described above (VIII, p. 116), he tried to hold the office by means of technicalities. But he was defeated, not only in his efforts to hold Project offices, but even in the internal workings of Unit 2 politics. Still aspiring to leadership, he began to inquire about delegates' duties and compensation and spoke of running at the next election, but this met with little interest.

Although neither Atcitty Jim nor Ray Johnson drank, even during the period of industrialization, other of Strong Man's sons did. Johnson Jones, a singer, often assaulted his wife after drinking parties and was arrested several times by tribal policemen. Kee Warner, one of Strong Man's own sons, drank more often but did not react so violently; during 1952 and 1953 he was arrested in town several times for drunkenness.

The family group of Hosteen Benally was the most stable in Strong Man's outfit. Hosteen Benally married Strong Man's older daughter but after about ten years of marriage was still childless. In his household lived his wife's widowed sister, her children, and three of Strong Man's children by his second wife. Their farm was well kept, in part because the entire field was in new alfalfa but also because the boys willingly helped mow, rake, and bale. Their 200 sheep were also herded by the children. With the farm chores well cared for, Hosteen Benally was able to spend full time working for the gas company after 1950; his pay was better than most, more than $2 an hour at one time, because he handled dynamite. On completion of the main pipeline, the company retained him for other types of work. Neither Hosteen Benally nor his wife spoke English. The youngest of the children living with them, however, went first to the Indian Service day school and then to the public school across the river.

CHAPTER XII

New Residents: Mike Cooper, Lawrence Willie, Carl Jackson

THOSE Fruitlanders who were "new" residents in the 1930's may be distinguished from most of their neighbors by their command of English, social relationships on the Project, tendency to acquire more non-Navaho material goods, enrollment of their children in either mission or public schools, ability over the years to find work with the government or with traders and farmers, and resultant greater experience in handling money. In the face of the changing situation the newcomers, too, made varying adjustments.

In a sense the newcomers had an advantage over the old residents when the economic situation changed. First, they had the advantage of living as separate biological families, without kinship extensions in the Project; they were not subjected to the strains of relationships within the extended family. Second, they were already geared to the cash economy; earning and spending money was no new experience. Third, having already oriented themselves toward the white man's culture, they became in a sense models for other Fruitlanders just beginning to emulate white men. With the boom of the 1950's, they achieved higher status.

Some newcomers, such as Mike Cooper and his family, made good adjustments both to the Fruitland community and to changes in the economic situation outside the Project. Others, Lawrence Willie and his family, for example, became disorganized. Still others remained aloof, as in the case of Carl Jackson. An individual personality, the environment in which he grew up, and the clarity with which he could understand situation, goals, and methods of achieving goals, all helped determine the success of his adjustment. Mike Cooper's career may thus be seen in the light of his tactfully limited participation through his first years on the Project. Lawrence Willie's head-on plunge into community affairs, by contrast, brought him only frustration. Carl Jackson's meeting of the situation, best defined in terms of his own passivity, eventually brought him greater satisfactions than those achieved by Lawrence Willie.

Mike Cooper was born around 1912 in Red Lake, New Mexico. His father, a former army scout, raised his children by white standards. Mike learned white ways at home and at the government school some twenty miles away; as soon as he had learned the fundamentals of English, he asked to attend the Sherman Institute at Riverside, California. Desiring further training, he went to the Haskell Institute at Lawrence, Kansas, where he learned how to service and repair gasoline and diesel motors, completing a three-year course in two years.

Mike returned to the reservation in 1935 and immediately obtained work with the government driving a tractor. After three years on this job, he moved to Fruitland and worked as an equipment operator. Except for a period in the armed forces, he was employed regularly at the Fruitland Project.

In 1937 he took a ten-acre assignment in Unit 1, four miles west of Farmington and five miles east of the government compound. He brought his wife and child to the Project in his 1932 Chevrolet sedan and settled them in a frame house that he had built himself. Their neighbors, wary of strangers at any time (like Navahos generally), considered the Coopers outsiders who had not joined in the movement to resist the change in land policy. Soon, however, the Coopers had the comfort of knowing other newcomers nearby. Whenever his children were ill or when his wife was in labor, Mike drove them to the mission hospital on the edge of town. Neither the Coopers nor other newcomers were asked to participate in the sings held for the sick among older residents.

In 1945 Mike was drafted. After three years in the Navy, he returned to his old job as tractor driver. He built the foundation for a new stone house. Once again old-timers in their round hogans gossiped about the Coopers' white ways. Although other neighbors had already built or were building the new rectangular homes, Mike's was far the best in design, construction, and materials. He roofed the house with asphalt paper and covered it with aluminum paint. Then he purchased beds, tables and chairs, a couch, and a large wood and coal range.

When he completed his house, he began to remodel the outbuildings, and he bought mechanized farm equipment—even though his full time was spent working for the government. When sent to operate machinery at other irrigation projects for a few weeks at a time, he could save some of his per diem for further purchases. (Mike's extra saving while away from home contrasted strongly with the tendency of many Navahos to spend all their entire income when away, leaving nothing for their families.)

In 1950 the Coopers, like a few other families with comparable background and interests, appeared quite contented with their way of life. They had refused to be disturbed by the old-timers' avoidance when they first arrived and were simply waiting until other Fruitlanders should orient themselves toward the white way before attempting to participate in community affairs. Neither Mr. nor Mrs. Cooper smoked; neither drank. Their life was centered in their home and their children. A new truck purchased in 1950 enabled them to make frequent weekend visits to their parents' homes.

The Coopers' house, larger than those of their neighbors, was used by missionaries as a meeting place, and now they and neighbors with like interests undertook new community activities of their own. Mrs. Cooper and her friends, all eager to apply in their own homes what they had learned in school, immediately asked an Indian Bureau home economist (added to the staff in 1951) to visit them. Soon they organized the first homemakers' club on the Project. One member of the club won the award for the best collection of home-garden produce at the Window Rock fair that year. The club represented the beginning of a concerted effort by the newcomers to participate in community affairs. Under their leadership, for example, bus service was secured for public school children.

By 1953 two of the Coopers' older boys were attending the Albuquerque Indian School. The older boy ranked high in his class scholastically and was also an athlete, competing in three different sports. He planned to attend college after a tour of duty in the Navy, and his father was prepared to help him financially. The younger children commuted daily to the public school eight miles from home and were active in the 4-H Club.

Lawrence Willie, about as old as Mike Cooper, had likewise had contact with whites all his life. Indeed, living with a white family when he was young and attending public school, he had learned to speak English fluently and had become familiar with many white patterns of life and thought. As a young adult, he lived a life less Navaho than white. His wife and his children all spoke English well.

In 1932, when Lawrence came to Fruitland, he had his first extensive contacts with Navahos. Government agents saw in him what they believed to be leadership qualities. In addition to his knowledge of English, he was informed about the national political situation, and he had expert skill in carpentry. He was given a position with the Civilian Conservation Corps as an interpreter, timekeeper, and general contact man between white and Navaho employees.

Soon after farms became available in Fruitland, Lawrence received an assignment and obtained a job with the Agency as a ditch rider. He put his skill as a carpenter to work immediately, built an adobe house, plastered the walls with stucco, and moved his family in. Thus, unlike the Coopers, who built their modern stone house only after the war, Lawrence was living according to non-Navaho standards in his first years at Fruitland. He was the first Navaho employee on the Irrigation Project to impose water regulation by setting the lateral gates with locks. Old residents regarded him with hostility, as following too closely the dictates of the government, though in time they would consider his ways as a subject for humor.

Before Lawrence's arrival at Fruitland, he was already a habitual drinker, and his persistent drinking soon cost him his government job. Now he left the Project for long periods, supporting himself at whatever jobs he could find. He returned to Fruitland only long enough to plant his crops but not to harvest them. During the war he rented his farm and home; later he stated that they were badly used.

After his war service in the Marine Corps, Lawrence attempted to re-establish himself at Fruitland. He lived with his wife and children and after 1950 worked in town. Although he drank and did not report for work regularly, he was an able enough man when sober to convince his employer that he should be rehired. On the Project, the many who increasingly believed that men with wide knowledge of the American scene should assume leadership positions succeeded in electing him to an office in the local chapter organization.

Lawrence plunged now into the task of developing a community organization to cope with the Fruitlanders' many problems. He spoke intelligently and tried to explain the white man's orientation. He gave considerable time at meetings to the discussion of community-development programs and outlined what he had read in the newspapers or heard over the radio. He initiated the move to get wells dug in both Units 1 and 3; and when they proved unusable because of the high alkaline content of the water, he and others called attention to the fact that Indian Service agents had ignored the recommendations of The People in locating the wells.

Another project which he tried to initiate was the building of a community house. He wanted the people to contribute labor, materials, and funds toward the building. But a mission-owned building already stood in the central location of Unit 1, and the missionary encouraged Fruitlanders to use the building for meetings and general social gatherings. In any event, the people generally did not respond to Lawrence's program as he hoped.

Because of his failure he became aggressive, particularly toward whites. He showed his lack of knowledge about Navaho culture and yet expressed some desire to defend it. "The white people come here and look at the Navahos and call them pagans," he said. "Let me tell you that the Navahos have only one God, it's the spirit. You white people have many Gods, and you never know which one to worship. We have only one God and it's the spirit." [1]

---

[1] Perhaps Lawrence felt that one religion could not safely be mentioned before the adherents of another. Asking one researcher, "What is your religion?" and getting the answer, "Catholic," he said, "Don't speak so loud, there are some Baptists here too."

He expressed hostility toward university people as well:

I know what university people are, no matter where they come from—Boston University, Harvard University, Cornell University, it is all the same. They are scientists, they try to explain everything by science, science is the only thing to them. They come here and dig holes and find some bones; they say they are Indian bones. Every time I would try to say something they would interrupt me and wouldn't let me have a chance to answer. White people come here and try to tell us what to do. The Indians are the only true Americans and they were here for a long time before the white people came. We should kick all the white people out of the reservation.

Having spent most of his life with non-Navahos, he had not internalized Navaho role behavior well enough to feel secure in it. Older residents who wanted to achieve the same goals were not to be hurried or pressured, nor were they sure what leadership such an unstable man could give. A circularity was established: Lawrence enthusiastically introduced and promoted suggestions; the people responded casually; Lawrence resented the lack of faith in his leadership. By 1953 he was complaining that his community office was unpaid: "Only the big shots, the people above me . . . get paid for what they do. Why should I work for my people and spend some money out of my own pocket? I didn't want that job, but they wanted me to be their headman, and to talk for them." His frustrations caused him to drink more and more. In 1953 and 1954 he was hospitalized several times following automobile accidents.

Carl Jackson, one of those who married into the Fruitland community, benefited by an assignment in Unit 2 but had to live within the narrow confines of the norms there, balancing as best he could between excessive exploitation by his neighbors and their gossip when he acted for himself. More accustomed to white ways than his neighbors in Unit 2, he found few Navahos with whom he could freely associate. He looked, accordingly, to white men as his companions. His wife had enough relatives in the unit to satisfy her need for companionship. Carl felt free of social pressures only after 1950.

Before Carl came to Fruitland in 1937 from Lukachukai, Arizona, he had attended the Shiprock boarding school and that at Albuquerque for six years. He had learned English and several trades, spent time with his white instructors, and discovered that he liked to visit town. There he looked at the windows, went to shows, and talked to white people. Carl's shyness was a social asset, for many whites seemed to like Indians better if they were not too aggressive.

When he returned to the reservation, he worked with a land-survey group. Weekends he went to town. Meeting a Fruitland girl employed there, he married her and went to live with her family in Unit 2, on a farm next to Atcitty Jim's. Carl's wife had learned to speak fluent English at the Shiprock school, as had her mother during the early 1900's. But their family life was in the traditional pattern.

Carl obtained an assignment in Unit 2. He secured farm help on his land in exchange for his own labor. At the same time, he found that he must contribute his labor and commodities to his wife's family without compensation—and that he was an outsider, with whom few persons of his own age group would associate. Perhaps as a result, he preferred to be with non-Navahos; he found that they liked his behavior, which they considered was "exceptional," "not smart aleck," "more white than Navaho." He found jobs at the store and as a fireman at the school. He enjoyed his work because it enabled him to read newspapers and magazines and to chat with the trader or the teachers. Yet at the same time he found his home life satisfying. He treated his many children, including his twin boys, kindly. He was generous toward his wife and respectful to his parents. And though usually punctual at work ("unusual among

Navahos," his employers said), he was independent and would not appear if he had work at home which he considered more pressing.

During World War II Carl served in the Marine Corps. Returning to Fruitland, he obtained a second farm of ten acres in Unit 3 and produced substantial yields but not as much as he expected. He had to travel to Unit 3 by wagon or on horseback, and he had to hire more labor. As long, however, as the wage rate (translated into commodities) was no more than that paid by white farmers, he was able to make a profit.

Carl's first experience with whites after he returned from service was unpleasant. Entering a bar and grill in civilian clothes, he asked for a sandwich but was refused service. When Carl threatened to break the showcases, the counterman prepared a sandwich for him. Carl paid, then told the counterman to throw it in the garbage. His acceptance by whites in the Marine Corps and elsewhere had left him unprepared for such discrimination.

When the gas company came into the area, Carl was forced to pay such high wages for farm labor that he could no longer make a profit. Although he could have secured local employment at once, for six months he worked at the sweetening plant of the El Paso Natural Gas Company located about three miles from his home rather than camp with the mobile pipelaying crews. (When he had earlier left home to work, his wife's relatives moved in and were of course both company and protection for his wife—but they did not leave readily on his return.)

When the sweetening plant was almost completed, Carl's foreman told him that he could continue to work either as a migrant pipeline laborer with overtime pay and realize over $450 a month or as a permanent maintenance man for the company housing project starting at $1.32 per hour. His foreman, his trader friend, and other white men whom he trusted urged him to accept the permanent position. Carl may have made the same decision even before consulting them.

As time passed, Carl began to feel more and more a part of the company. Although at first a little disappointed because he was not assigned a position in the sweetening plant itself, he was soon gratified to receive from the personnel office the same packet of printed and mimeographed literature given to white employees. The literature included information about the company and its employment policies—the deductions for unemployment and hospitalization insurance, various benefits, and especially the employee's opportunity to purchase stocks. Carl again asked his fellow employees' advice about the benefits and about becoming a stockholder. He began to purchase stock through the company's payroll-deduction plan.

Now that most able-bodied men in Unit 2 worked for wages as high as Carl's, he was rarely asked for money. Although he tended his farm when he could, his harvest did not exceed other farmers', and he was not asked to contribute from his crops. His wife's family came only occasionally to baby-sit. He bought a car; several times a week he took his family to movies. On Saturdays he went into town to purchase clothing and to take his sons at the mission school to the movies or to ball games. He gave his younger children various toys, including bicycles. He added furnishings to his home. He planned, too, to replace his frame and tar-paper structure with a six-room cinder-block house.[2] He spent many hours examining blueprints given him by the gas-company contractor.

Since Carl's arrival in Fruitland during the late 1930's he had visited his own parents only at rare intervals, for although they

[2] His present home, just off the main road which ran to Unit 3 and through most of Unit 2, was a convenient stopping-off point for drunks; during the early hours of the morning they woke Carl and his family to ask if they could spend the night lest they be thrown out by members of their own families, or to beg for his intercession in quarrels, or to ask for help in pulling their cars out of the irrigation canal.

lived only fifty miles away, thirty of those miles were over
reservation roads, with no public transportation available. Once
during the late 1940's his parents visited him, and again in 1951.
Now that he had his own car, he could visit them more often.

The relationship between Carl and his wife was non-Navaho
in pattern. Carl earned the money to support the family; his
wife took care of the house, the children, and the minor chores
in the garden. Although Carl sometimes went to squaw dances
by himself or with friends, he took his wife and occasionally his
older children to the movies. By purchase of various household
furnishings, Carl attempted to lighten his wife's work load and
to make his family comfortable. Even before he worked for the
gas company, he had bought a gas-operated washing machine.
Their house, although small for so large a family, was furnished
with beds, chairs, table, radio, and coal range.

With the whole community in rapid transition from the
Navaho to the white way, Carl's isolated position was no longer
a liability. The stresses which troubled most members of extended families did not affect Carl, for he had already made the
adjustment. Unlike Junior and Jerry Begay and Bob and Pete
Johnson, Carl looked almost exclusively to non-Navahos for
guidance. Indeed, he seemed to desire their respect more than
that of his own people.

CHAPTER XIII

Conclusion

THE foregoing analysis of the Fruitland Navahos has focused upon technological, social, and economic change stemming both from directed programs and from economic and political developments throughout region and nation. This final chapter will (1) summarize the change process as perceived at Fruitland, (2) draw some general principles which may be applicable to future programing both for Navahos and in other underdeveloped areas, and (3) consider the current Navaho program in the light of the present situation.

The new canal system forced the Navahos into a cash economy. Although a vast improvement over the two previous irrigation systems, it still created many tensions. The new system could have given old residents larger acreages. But this was not the policy, for larger acreages would have been contrary to the Navahos' traditional farming practices. Furthermore, there was a need to rehabilitate many other Indians who were deprived of livelihood by the stock-reduction program.[1] In addition, subsistence farming was being advocated as a way

[1] See Spicer, "Sheepmen and Technicians," in *Human Problems in Technological Change*, pp. 185–207.

of life by the Department of Agriculture for all people during the depression.

The announced policy of the Indian Service was to introduce new technology in the framework of the "Navaho cultural and economic system." However, the Indian Service deviated from this and drastically altered the social structure by bringing into the Project new people, leveling off economic status by equalizing land and sheep holdings, and distributing plots without consideration of the Navaho kinship pattern. On the other hand, the Navajo Indian Agency adhered to the notion of "meshing objectives with the values and social organization of the Navaho" by continuing to frame the program as though the reservation were a cultural island. Evidence of this are to be seen in the Indian Bureau's policy during the Collier administration.[2]

World War II created further strains. After a short period of hesitation Fruitlanders responded in great numbers to recruiters for off-reservation labor and for the armed forces. In addition to such factors as the generally loose structure of Navaho society and the high value placed on warrior status,[3] at Fruitland the problem of making a living also loomed large. The low productivity of their farms forced many Navahos to seek work away from the reservation. Their absence from the Project, together with the heterogeneity of the residents, forestalled development of an over-all social organization necessary to control the Project's water distribution, to enforce land use, and to serve as a medium through which agricultural methods could be taught.

During the war years and until 1950, two simultaneous processes created strains but at the same time helped the Fruit-

[2] E. R. Fryer, "Navajo Social Organization and Land Use Adjustment," *Scientific Monthly,* LV (1942), 415–422.

[3] John Adair and Evon Z. Vogt, "Navaho and Zuni Veterans: A Study of Contrasting Modes of Culture Change," *American Anthropologist,* n.s. LI (1949), 547–562.

landers prepare themselves for the industrial boom which came to the San Juan Valley in late 1950. First, there was considerable off-reservation experience for a sizable segment of the Fruitland population, including the "long-hair" traditionalists. Second, life on the reservation held fewer opportunities for transmission, perpetuation, and strengthening of the native culture. (Yet gossip and other sanctions still kept the progressives from assuming leadership positions.) Off-reservation work weakened the culture at home. Fathers were no longer available to tell the traditional stories. With children away at school they had little opportunity to learn their cultural roles through daily interactions with family members.

In 1950 the El Paso Natural Gas Company entered the area and gave employment to over eighty Fruitland farmers, while many others secured positions in Farmington, the expanding town close by. The Navahos' response seemed to indicate that they now saw the situation as changed.[4] Thus many latent roles which the Navahos had already learned elsewhere were now manifested at home. It was apparent from the field data, however, that these roles had not been well learned,[5] and some disastrous effects resulted from the sudden general affluence of the population.

The first effect of widespread work opportunities in the vicinity was the creation of a cash surplus which enabled the Navahos to make down payments on pickup trucks. Mobility in turn led to further breakdown in the social organization. Co-operation broke down even in Unit 2, where the social

[4] See Edmund H. Volkhart, *Social Behavior and Personality* (New York: Social Science Research Council, 1951), p. 117.

[5] Vogt observed in his *Navaho Veterans*, p. 117, that the process of shifting values from Navaho to white involves first an "imitative 'stage'" in which selected value patterns of the dominant society are imitated but not internalized. At a much later date in the acculturation process, a more fundamental shift occurs in which white values begin to be *internalized*." The two stages, "imitative" and "internalized," apply equally well in the case of role learning.

organization had most closely resembled the traditional pattern. Individuals could not apply pressures on relatives or neighbors for assistance. Excuses for not helping now became acceptable, and it was easy for families to leave at a moment's notice, either to go to trading posts or to town, in order to avoid co-operating with neighbors and relatives.

Wagework and ownership of cars had other ramifications in the community. Ceremonials, until now normally held at the convenience of the patients' families or relatives of the medicine man, were scheduled over weekends to suit the convenience of wageworkers. At the same time, automobiles and surplus cash made it possible for Navahos to obtain wine and bring it to the sings; there was much drinking among participants and visitors. The more conservative believed that such behavior upset the basic premises of Navaho religion.

Because Fruitlanders were now purchasing cars on the installment plan, they could not afford to lose their jobs by being absent. Accordingly, whenever they became ill they avoided long convalescence by going to white doctors for "shots," sometimes with the encouragement of the medicine men themselves. The ready acquisition of cash and mobility changed the Fruitlanders' general spending habits. Whereas in the past they had established credit at one store and paid for their purchases with crops or cash from livestock sales, now they bought freely in town until they had exhausted their ready cash, went next to ask for credit at the trading posts, and then on payday, instead of paying their debts, made more purchases in town. Traders at first criticized the Navahos for such practices but ended by remodeling posts and services in order to compete.

Although wagework experience disturbed some English-speaking Navahos, in general their position in the community improved. Now they could interpret for non-English-speaking fellow workers. With most traditionally minded Fruitlanders working sixty or more hours a week and hence unable to conduct regular community affairs, the younger men and their wives met together a little less formally, to set up a new chapter organization and to petition the government for water wells and for school buses.

From the highlights of the change process, some general propositions emerged, many of them common knowledge to social scientists and to administrators, others perhaps new or varying slightly from previous concepts of change programs. These propositions are on a first level of approximation—not rigidly tested, but serviceable as guidelines for the personnel of technological aid programs. The assumption is explicit that communities all over the world are in a process of transition from one to another type of community, whether with or without directed programs. Leighton and Smith, in a comparative study of change, found that four patterns appeared to be common to each of seven communities in widely separated parts of the world (of which Fruitland was one):

(1) A trend away from an economic system that was primarily self-contained and independent, towards a cash economy with dependence on a larger social group such as a state or the nation.

(2) A similar shift in governmental and political affairs from relative local autonomy to dependence on higher authority in the larger social group.

(3) Changes in values, ideologies, and social usages. These changes, although they constitute a break with the traditional and are increasingly influenced by outside forces, are not altogether in harmony with the economic and governmental trends noted above, or consistent with each other within a given community.

(4) Progressive secularization of life, with an increasingly sharp line drawn between religious and other human activities such as work, government, and recreation.[6]

[6] Alexander H. Leighton and Robert J. Smith, "A Comparative Study of Social and Cultural Change," *Proceedings of the American Philosophical Society*, XCIX (1955), 81.

These processes serve as the context for the propositions which follow.

1. Change is a multidimensional concept. Two dimensions which are particularly meaningful for personnel involved in technological aid programs are the rate of change process and its extent.[7] This proposition appears to be so obvious that its mention may be superfluous. Yet, perhaps because it is so obvious, there has been some neglect of the important part which an understanding of it can play in directed change programs.

As for rate of change, three of many aspects may be remarked: fluctuation over time, variations within the population, and variations among aspects of culture. First, social and cultural change appears to fluctuate in its rate over time. At one period changes may occur at a tremendous speed, and at another period they occur so slowly as to give the culture an appearance of being static. At Fruitland, it has been evident, changes in the social structure appeared slowly until the government constructed the new canal system and relocated many families. Change accelerated as new farms were assigned exclusively to men, and later change accelerated as the result of the war, off-reservation work, and wagework in the vicinity.

Fruitland has also illustrated how rate of change varies by age levels, sex, and interest groups. The young have tended to accept change more rapidly than old people whose habits are more fixed, though at the same time some old people have demonstrated modern ideas, if not for themselves, then for their children or grandchildren. Vogt has suggested that men, because of their wider firsthand contact with the outside world and their mobility, acculturate faster than the women.[8] At the same time Rapoport has found that Navaho women tend to accept Christianity more readily than do men.[9] And with regard to

[7] *Ibid.*, p. 82.   [8] Vogt, *Navaho Veterans*, p. 93.
[9] Rapoport, *Changing Navaho Religious Values*, p. 72.

groups which cut across age and sex lines, the central tribal government, for example, has adjusted to new opportunities much faster than local officers.

Another facet of rate of change is the varying rate by aspects of culture. For the Navaho the material aspect of life has seemed to change more rapidly than the nonmaterial. Yet within the Navaho system itself there is some evidence that under certain circumstances the ideological can change with great rapidity; for example, the function of the singers seems threatened because of Navahos' increased involvement in the non-Navaho world.

The above three aspects of rate of change must be viewed not in a vacuum but in some sort of context. Changes within a sociocultural group may proceed at a slower or faster rate, depending upon the situation. A spurt in population growth may begin to outstrip the natural resources of the settlement area; or technology may not be advanced to the point at which it can cope with floods or other natural catastrophes. The belief system may hamper the people's adaptation to the changing environment. And the degree of contact experience and the circumstances of that experience may govern the rate of change.

The second dimension of change is its extent or its ramification in the socioculture. Because the components of a culture are interdependent, one might suppose that a change in one part automatically affects all other segments in it. Such an ideal state does not exist in reality, but it serves as a useful model for examining societies. Depending upon what the innovations are, they may predictably have more or less extended ramifications in the community. The mission influenced Fruitland through its health services but barely touched the people in a religious sense. On the other hand, wagework affected almost everyone in the community and all aspects of the socioculture including religion. The irrigation system was another innovation which affected not only the long-established residents but also those who had migrated into the Project.

2. The speed and extent of changes may bring about disorganization in the community. "Disruption of customs, communication, authority systems, cooperation, and shared values" may result when "a given society" faces innovations exceeding its "threshold of tolerance for change." [10] For the administrator's purpose, then, introduction of changes must be geared not only to the rate of change already existing in the society or culture, but to its tolerance for stress. Changes even of a beneficent nature can be damaging if applied at too great a speed. Thus in Fruitland, after 1950, the Indians suddenly became affluent at the very time of other drastic changes: the repeal of the federal law which had prohibited sale of liquor to Indians, increased welfare aid, increased education for children, and increased face-to-face contact with non-Navahos in the vicinity. In spite of some experience in non-Navaho behavior, events came too swiftly for the Fruitlanders to acquire and understand new habit patterns well. Like many white men, they could not yet manage money wisely; they had to learn through trial and error how much liquor they could handle; they had to discover channels through which they could get welfare aid; they needed a clearer conception of the role of education; and they still had to gain assurance in the presence of non-Navahos.

The impacts were also too rapid for the Fruitlanders to adjust their pre-existing social organization to the newly created situation. Informal as well as institutional patterns of social control broke down. Drinking became rampant at sings and squaw dances; young people married clan mates; co-operative work on farms lost its place; transmission of Navaho culture from old to young and relationships among members of the kinship groups deteriorated. To be sure, replacements in cultural

[10] Leighton and Smith, "A Comparative Study of Social and Cultural Change," pp. 82–83.

behavior were sanctioned by tribal and local leaders: policemen now controlled deviant behavior; marriage certificates at the county courthouse replaced traditional ceremonies; farmers helped each other for wages; boarding schools took care of the education of children; and members of the biological family became closer to each other. But such replacements did not fill many of the gaps which the new situation had created.

3. Knowledge of the pre-existent sociocultural system and its quality must be complemented by knowledge of the direction of changes. With such knowledge, the administrator can decide whether he should try to inject the new item into the old pattern—which, though currently present, might be disappearing—or whether he should encourage the new—which, though currently weak, is emerging. This notion is far removed from the traditional orientation of persons who have been involved in programs of directed culture change. Actually it builds upon earlier notions. A brief history of the development of ideas on this score appears to have been as follows.

The "most simple" idea of directed culture change, still widely current, is that a government agent or a missionary goes into an alien culture equipped with superior knowledge wherewith he may educate the "ignorant." He hopes that the recipients will take cognizance of his superiority and accept his introductions. Responses to such an approach have varied from grateful change to antagonistic rejection and cannot be predicted.

A more sophisticated concept, stemming from the knowledge that anthropology has brought to administration, assumes that, though a technological advance may help a people, yet because their culture is a totality of interdependent parts it is naturally resistant to changes which may create stress and strains in its various components and that consequently the layout of the sociocultural system must be studied to determine what can be introduced and where the new idea can be injected. Theoretically, such analysis will make possible a successful change with a minimum of disruption. This was the broad framework of the federal Navaho program which began during the 1930's.

The Fruitland Irrigation Project was part of this Indian Service program. It was concerned with the conservation of natural resources and with the improvement of human life. The superintendent at that time wrote:

The desperate efforts of a people, with a simple technology, to fill their bellies and clothe themselves and their children may produce a dust bowl. The spiritual values of the people who dignify the heavens and the earth as living human beings may place barriers in the way of doing what appears to be reasonable and practical. The values, aptitudes and mechanical habits of the people may hasten or retard conservation and human rehabilitation.

In order to approach these problems in a humane way, he advocated that the government mesh its "objectives with the values and social organization of the Navajo." [11]

Although this conceptualization may have been satisfactory for such small improvements as were made on the aboriginal irrigation systems during the 1920's, the problems which faced the Indian Service in the late 1930's were far more complex than the administrator realized. Three general groups of complicating factors, already described in these pages, were a new approach to Indian administration, the economic depression and the onset of World War II, and a population increase which further taxed the reservation's resources.

As a result, certain weaknesses underlay the second-level notions about change programs (and suggest a third approach). In the Navaho program during the 1930's there was emphasis on meshing the administration's goals with the values of the recipient culture, a meshing not always carried out in operation but nevertheless the ideal of the policy maker. In addition, the

[11] Fryer, "Navajo Social Organization and Land Use Adjustment," pp. 409–410.

Navaho reservation was considered as a cultural island. But as has appeared constantly in these pages, the Navahos, like many other cultural groups, have been subjected to strains brought about by natural catastrophe, economic shifts beyond their control, political upheaval, and population increase. Focusing only upon problems within the boundaries of the reservation, the Indian Service overlooked factors of tremendous import which had their roots in the larger society, the region, and the nation. The government had thought of its course of action as geared to an emergency situation. The program, considering the situation both within and outside the reservation which emerged under these conditions, was incompatible with longer-term trends. No one, of course, could tell how long the economic depression or the drought would continue. But, to say the least, the situation was not normal.

In addition, although the Indian Service visualized and planned longer-term projects, the planners neglected the time dimension. Large-scale construction is accomplished only over several years. Irrigation work was initiated during the mid-1930's and completed a few years before another abnormal period, World War II. During this period the philosophy of subsistence farming continued as the guiding principle. In other words, plans designed for a previous situation were no longer realistic. The goal of establishing subsistence farming as a way of life was in conflict with the cash economy of which the Indians were now so clearly a part. The planners should have anticipated, through integrated application of the various social sciences, what the social and cultural situation would be like when the project was completed.

4. Directed technological change projects must be viewed as part of a greater whole. Although various facets of this proposition have already been discussed, it is introduced here specifically to make apparent the interdependence of the Fruitland Project with the most extended political, economic, and

social environment. These links are of various forms and intensities. Some relationships may be intimate and immediate; other links tangential and distant. The Fruitlanders' situation has been seen as characterized by many such extensions or linkages. Indeed, the influence of these links may have been greater than that of directed technological change, though sometimes no direct manifestations of behavioral changes appeared to result, at least until the situation changed still further.

Three groups need to know that the change project is part of the greater whole—the administrators, the specific recipients of the program, and the people of the region involved generally. The administrators must prepare the goals of their projects so that they will integrate with the external linkages. The planning should include the involved people so that they too will have an understanding of their own roles in the larger regional and national setting. And the population which comprises the context of the aid project must know about it as a reciprocal context for their own economic and social development. A co-ordinated approach such as this is difficult and expensive, demanding skills and perspectives which few men possess. The Indian Service has gone far in achieving this objective. It has developed, through the long period of refining by highly sensitive personnel, a capable and responsible tribal leadership structure. It has carried through an educational program to which the Navaho people have responded vigorously. But in the process wide gaps have been unintentionally created. Leadership is well developed to integrate tribal objectives with those of the outside world, but followers at the grass roots are still lacking. Education proceeds rapidly for children, but there are too few programs for men and women still young and vigorous but too old for formal education. Education is preparing youngsters for livelihood away from the reservation, but the world outside is not yet prepared to accept them as equals.

5. Enthusiasm for changes should be harnessed and guided

to avoid repercussions leading to instabilities in social organization and individual personality. As Leighton suggests,

communities under stress, with their labile but intense emotions and shifting systems of belief, are ripe for change. While this is a situation fraught with danger because of trends which may make the stress become worse before it gets better, there is also an opportunity for administrative action that is not likely to be found in more secure times. Skillful administration may be able to seize the moment not only to guide spontaneous shifts in constructive directions, but even to achieve extensive changes that would otherwise be impossible or extremely difficult.[12]

But in such situations there is a tendency for people to accept any ready means to ends which have been defined and accepted by them but not always by others involved. For example, as mentioned earlier, great enthusiasm has been generated among the Navahos for education for their children. Education is looked upon as the panacea which will cure their ills. The people who are voicing concern over the replacement of Navaho culture with white man's ways are in the minority. Yet there are troublesome ramifications to the diffusion of white education, which some old Navahos discern much more sophisticatedly than do learned educators. Not only do young Navahos at school lose that Navaho culture which has given their people a sense of security in the past, but in the isolated and segregated school situation they gain little real understanding of white culture. Although boarding schools do a very adequate job of teaching Navaho children how to get on in the school situation, of preparing them for semiskilled and unskilled jobs, of furnishing them some degree of social grace for the world outside the campus and the reservation, all this is only questionable preparation for the shock that they must face when they compete in the world outside. They are insecure in

[12] Alexander H. Leighton, *The Governing of Men* (Princeton: Princeton University Press, 1945), p. 359.

their knowledge both of their own culture and of the white man's. (In 1957 the Navaho began to be integrated into the New Mexico school system.)

Another panacea currently looked to as a means of rehabilitating the Navahos is industry; in the rapidly developing Southwest there is great opportunity for placing Indians in new industries. In order to draw industry the Tribal Council in 1956 appropriated $300,000 to be used toward building construction or the programing of on-the-job training in any industrial firm which would use Navaho manpower.[13] The gulf between the Navahos' present understanding of an expected behavior under industrial conditions is wide and must be bridged with a comprehensive educational program which will make meaningful the experiences that they have already had in off-reservation industrial work. The program should not only reorient their present norms to those predictable in industry, but reorient them in such a way as not to destroy completely The People's own cultural values. The Navahos must also learn how to use their own native resources and institutions in the greater society which will give them a full life. To ignore these intervening variables would almost automatically lead to Navaho maladjustment, discontent, apathy, and further mistrust of government, not to mention the strengthening of the belief among white men that the Indian is an inferior sort of being. Linton's statement regarding the dealings of Indians with the United States government is much to the point.

Tribe after tribe made a real effort to copy white ways when they were placed on reservations. They saw the old life was ended and did their best to adapt. However, whenever a tribe got a communally owned cattle herd which could be a valuable source of income, stockmen who wanted the range brought pressure in Washington, and the tribe suddenly found its herd sold and the money "put in trust." If a tribe developed an irrigation project and brought new land under cultivation, presently an excuse would be found for

[13] *Farmington Daily Times,* Dec. 9, 1955.

expropriating this and moving the tribe to a still more sub-marginal territory. The Indians were frustrated and puzzled by changing government policies, in which the only consistent feature was that they always lost, and finally settled into apathy and pauperism.[14]

In many ways the current policy which attempts to assimilate the Indians into the mainstream of American life appears to have undertones of the past. The motives of the white man appear to be the same, although some are different. Uranium, oil, and irrigation projects are to be found on the Navaho reservation. Such a policy of compulsory assimilation as that attempted by the Indian Service when it was transferred from the War Department in 1849 might have disastrous repercussions on the Navahos, even though they are themselves the foremost proponents of the need for a new way of life. Thompson formulates the forced assimilation policy succinctly:

The program, which led to the development of a complicated bureaucracy, included: (1) the wasting of tribal resources by making concessions of Indian lands to non-Indian for farming, mining, and grazing, by wholesale deforestation of Indian lands; and by neglect of measures to insure conservation of resources; (2) the fractionization of Indian Tribal land by their compulsory allotment in severalty and descent to heirs; (3) the forcing of children to attend government military boarding schools continuously throughout their formative years; (4) the banning of the various Indian religions and their ceremonial expressions and the encouragement and subsidization of Christian missionaries to proselyte in Indian schools and on Indian lands; (5) the deliberate discrediting of Indian values, language, arts, and morality in Indian schools, on the Reservations, and in government reports to Congress and the general public.[15]

[14] Ralph Linton, "Cultural and Personality Factors Affecting Economic Growth," in Bert F. Hoselitz, ed., *The Progress of Underdeveloped Areas* (Chicago: University of Chicago Press, copyright 1952 by the University of Chicago), p. 76.
[15] Laura Thompson, *Culture in Crisis* (New York: Harper & Brothers, 1950), p. 144.

6. A convergence is crucially necessary in the definition of the situation by the various groups involved—and most difficult to achieve—for systems of beliefs are not easy to change. As Leighton suggests, "in producing remedial changes in a community, it is necessary to take into consideration the fact that people are moved by appeals to the feeling man more than to the rational man. . . . The administrator's job is to accept these things as they are and to take them into consideration, turn them to advantage if possible, but never ignore them." [16] Even in the white society, basic beliefs hinder convergence with regional changes in the socioeconomic development, as Vogt found in his study of the homesteaders in New Mexico.[17]

Other difficulties, however, stem from the failure to use existing means adequately and the cognitive component of beliefs. Heavy emphasis on improving communication, for example, is one way of helping to bring about convergence. This is not easy, as the Fruitland situation has illustrated. In a transitional society, the members of which must refer to many group norms, some of them contradictory, the difficulties appear insurmountable. In this sort of complex situation traditional, transitional, and modern methods of communication must be relied upon so as to establish links with all groups. Three questions may serve as a start toward finding ways of improving upon the situation. What are the existing channels of communication? What are the principal blocks which prevent information from being adequately communicated? What are the alternative ways of getting information to people?

At Fruitland, various blockages were seen as created by the structure of the society and by cultural differences. Among others, there were cleavages brought about by the immigration of new residents, the absence of residents from the Project

---

[16] Leighton, *The Governing of Men*, p. 361.
[17] Evon Z. Vogt, *The Modern Homesteaders* (Cambridge: Harvard University Press, 1955).

through much of the year, and the disintegration of the social organization as a result of rapid changes. Under these circumstances it was not possible to rely upon traditional channels exclusively, nor was it profitable to communicate with the people through the traders, for news items were not always brought to the attention of the Indians. But these means were used to some extent, as well as others to be mentioned presently.

Besides the social-structure problem, there was the language difference. The channels of communication between people at the grass roots and the Tribal Council, particularly, were blocked for this reason. Reams of memoranda, policy statements, and minutes of meetings were written in the English language and so served no useful purpose when councilmen who could not read English returned home to make their reports. The same problem also affected federal agents in their relations with the Indians, quite apart from their lack of knowledge of Navaho ways. They found it easier to establish relations with English-speaking Navahos who were often out of touch with most of their own society. Thus the agents divorced themselves further from the community at large and often put additional strains on the English-speaking tribesmen in their community relationships.

Within the Agency there were also structural reasons for blockages. Because of the magnitude of the Agency's operation, the personnel of each branch, immersed in their own problems, tended to lose sight of over-all aims. At the higher levels the problem was perhaps not so noticeable, for staff meetings were held regularly; but communications often broke down between Washington or Window Rock and field personnel, as well as among the field agents themselves. Although formal channels of communication existed, directives, policy statements, and the minutiae were mislaid or unintentionally ignored because of more pressing problems.

Some steps have been taken to facilitate communication

among the Indians themselves and among the agency personnel. The aim is toward establishing means to get more agreement in the perceptions which various groups have about the Navaho rehabilitation program. In the southeastern part of the reservation Tribal Council news in the Navaho language can be heard over the local radio station. Although other border towns also have broadcasting studios, this public-service feature has not gained foothold. But many stations now broadcast Navaho-language programs several times daily, and the Indians have opportunities to listen to newscasts as well as to Navaho and cowboy music. Within the Agency, contacts via short-wave radio and more frequent staff meetings at the field level have helped to clear up some misunderstandings.

7. To prevent the chaos consequent upon too rapid changes, the effort to help people adjust must be of the same magnitude as the forces which create the changes. All too often the human aspects of large-scale projects are minimized or entirely neglected, whether in projects sponsored by private enterprise or in those of governmental bodies. Directed projects on the scale anticipated for the Navahos, as well as those in progress all over the world, involve the lives of many more people than live in the immediate vicinity. Even such a project as that at Fruitland, embracing only 2,500 acres, created strains which prevented its proper functioning for years. The strains in human relationships as exemplified on the Fruitland Project are tiny indeed when projected against the Navajo Project, which will relocate 1,900 families, or against the Damodar Irrigation Project in India or developments elsewhere in the world.

Such programs touch upon some of the basic concepts which have been developed in the social sciences. The main question to be answered is, Given a basic program or direction of change perceived to be good, or inevitable, by the people involved, what can the social sciences contribute to humanize the change process? The problem then becomes twofold. First, concepts and theories must be refined and new ones developed and incorporated into the program, which is designed to help indigenous peoples make the transition from an old to a different way of life. Besides those propositions developed here, such concepts as "shared values," [18] "dominant and substitute profiles of cultural orientations," [19] reference-group theory,[20] manifest and latent function,[21] communication theory,[22] and role theory [23] might be tested in the action frame of reference. Second, social scientists will have to be trained to use these theories in the context of real-life field situations. They will have to be selected and trained to work closely with administrators and indigenous people so that not only practical but scientific results will be obtained.

The future for Fruitlanders must be considered in the light of predictions for the San Juan area and for New Mexico and the Southwest generally. Ralph L. Edgel, director of the Bureau of Business Research in the College of Business Administration, University of New Mexico, states:

National trends cause an ebb and flow of the business tides of New Mexico. But recent years have shown us that the ebb is usually not as extreme in New Mexico as in the nation generally, and the upsurge is even greater in this state than in the rest of America. This is be-

[18] David F. Aberle, "Shared Values in Complex Societies," *American Sociological Review*, XV (1950), 495–502.

[19] Florence R. Kluckhohn, "Dominant and Substitute Profiles of Cultural Orientations: Their Significance for the Analysis of Social Stratification," *Social Forces*, XXVIII (1950), 376–393.

[20] Robert K. Merton and Alice S. Kitt, "Contributions to the Theory of Reference Group Behavior," in Robert K. Merton and Paul F. Lazarsfeld, eds., *Continuities in Social Research* (Glencoe, Ill.: Free Press, 1950), pp. 40–105.

[21] Merton, *Social Theory and Social Structure*, ch. i.

[22] Charles E. Osgood, "The Nature and Measurement of Meaning," *Psychological Bulletin*, XLIX (1952), 197–237.

[23] Leonard S. Cottrell, Jr., "The Adjustment of the Individual to His Age and Sex Roles," *American Sociological Review*, VII (1942), 617–620.

cause New Mexico is one of the few economic frontiers in the country, and development is both needed and welcomed. Each year brings new gains that tend to remain even when the business tide turns.[24]

The potentialities in the northwest corner of the state are virtually untapped in spite of the recent upsurge in economic development.

An official of the El Paso Natural Gas's refining subsidiary told the *Wall Street Journal* in mid-April that the Company is undecided about how large the new Wingate refinery [now completed] should be. He said, "They are discovering oil so fast in the area that we don't know how much is going to be produced from there a year from now."

. . . In any case, the crude oil refinery and gathering system will undoubtedly encourage more exploration and drilling of the Four Corners area. The San Juan Basin is thrice blessed: first with gas, then uranium, and now oil! [25]

But as great as the potentialities are for the development of extractive industries, one basic ingredient, water, is still lacking. Recent legislation to authorize the construction of the Navajo Dam, which is located about thirty miles east of Farmington, as part of the Upper Colorado River Storage Project indicates, however, that this natural resource also may be tapped.

The growth of Farmington and the San Juan Basin under the impact of the Navajo Dam and the Upper Colorado River Storage Project has been declared unbounded. . . . It was only recently that Victor T. Johnston, consulting engineer for Utah Construction, told the *Daily Times* that Navajo Dam would assure his company of a firm water supply for the proposed steam-electric plant and subsidiary petrochemical plants in . . . the Kirtland-Fruitland area. He

[24] *New Mexico Business* (Bureau of Business Research, College of Business Administration, University of New Mexico), IX (Feb., 1956), 4.
[25] *Ibid.*, IX (April, 1956), 4.

said Utah definitely planned to build as soon as allied industries were determined that would use portions of the vast power output.[26]

Construction of the Navajo Dam, besides bringing 115,000 acres of reservation land into cultivation and thus enabling 1,900 families to raise their standard of living to that of white people who have irrigated land, would enable another 2,200 families to earn their living through enterprises supported directly by agriculture.[27] Contingent upon action by Congress, realization of the programs may take as long as fifteen years. Whites as well as Navahos are expected to benefit from the program. Some 29,000 acres of nonreservation land will be put under irrigation. Water from the Navajo Dam will be diverted from the San Juan River to supply the demands of the growing population in the Middle Rio Grande Valley.

Within this framework, the prospects for the Fruitlander's future may be discussed in terms of (1) the shift in the power position of the Navaho Tribal Council and The People as a whole, (2) the history of intercultural relations in the valley, and (3) the government's approach to the problem.

One of the most striking changes to take place in the recent history of the Navahos is an increase, which has not yet been widely recognized, in the power position of the Tribal Council and of The People. So far the Council has wielded influence in the field of intercultural relations only when large business concerns have come on the reservation—for example, in the number of concessions made to the Navahos when the pipeline was put across reservation land. Only a few years ago the affairs of the Tribal Council were largely run by government officials. Today the councilmen are responsible, through their

[26] *Farmington Daily Times*, March 6, 1956, p. 9.

[27] *Ibid.*, July 22, 1954; *The Navajo Yearbook of Planning in Action*, Report no. V, 1955, p. 21; *The Navajo Yearbook*, Report no. VI, Fiscal Year 1957, pp. 92–93.

own tribal organization, for business transactions amounting to millions of dollars annually. Navahos contribute heavily to the economic livelihood of the region. Towns along U.S. Highway 66 have long profited from their trade with Indians. A study completed in 1954 reveals that the volume of trade which the Indians brought to the town of Gallup was 31 per cent of its total sales, or about $8,500,000. The present volume of Navaho trade in the San Juan Valley is perhaps not as large as that found in towns located along Highway 66, but potentially it is greater, as has been recognized by local civic leaders attempting to bring about the realization of the Navajo Dam.

Although the passage of the Upper Colorado River Basin Storage Project bill has been linked closely with politics, nevertheless the people of New Mexico through newspaper reports have been constantly made aware of the role of the Navaho as the key figure in their fight for water. The Navahos' rights have been used as leverages to get more water for New Mexico. Thus the Aztec Chamber of Commerce, in a letter to the President of the United States, wrote:

But we speak not merely to serve ourselves. In the treaty of 1868 the United States granted to the Navaho Indians a prior claim to the waters which flow past their Reservation. When it comes to honoring agreements with Indian tribes the record of the United States is not one to be proud of. . . . The Government has but two choices—to provide the Navaho with a decent basic economy, through making available the water to which they are entitled, or to face the necessity with its accompanying shame, of another treaty broken, of placing them on a perpetual dole.[28]

The brunt of the campaign for passage of the bill has rested in the hands of a few, but in 1954 the "grass roots" were being tapped. Thus, besides the $39,000 budget which the Upper Colorado Commission appropriated as one phase of "an eight

[28] *Farmington Daily Times*, Dec. 26, 1954.

point program calling for newspaper, motion picture and magazine publicity in an all out effort of the commission to bring enactment" by the 84th Congress, an organization named Aqualantes was formed "as a 'grass roots' organization." It was created to allow every person in the four upper-basin states to participate in the program and to push the storage bill in Congress. The then chairman of the Tribal Council, Sam Ahkeah, as a member of the executive committee and with consent from the Council, appropriated $10,000 to this fund.[29]

Navaho and non-Navaho leaders have a fairly good understanding of many of the major problems involved in the politics of getting bills passed in Congress. To some extent, because of widespread publicity given the Navajo Dam in newspapers, average citizens in New Mexico have also become better informed, but most remain unconcerned about the problems of Navaho adjustment in their world. More dramatic is the gap which exists between Window Rock—the Tribal Council and the Navajo Service—and the local Navahos. The Tribal Council members may be cognizant of well-laid plans and of the Navahos' involvement in the resource development on and near their reservation, but local presentation of such matters would require prodigious feats of memory. As a result the local people remain uninformed, and therefore unconcerned.

Affluence and political power must go hand in hand with education in the context of the total situation. Otherwise, what could be considered assets to the general welfare of The People may turn out to be liabilities. Thus recent moves to get Indian children into public schools in border towns, enabling them to gain early positive experiences in the white world, have also exposed them to many traumatic experiences. In this regard a preliminary study [30] of the adjustment of Navahos to town life in Farmington is instructive. In town, parents have little control

[29] *Ibid.*
[30] Seymour Parker and Tom T. Sasaki, unpublished manuscript, 1953.

over their children. Children find that their parents cannot provide the material possessions that their white schoolmates have, and the parents' prestige is further lowered in their children's eyes by their relative inability to speak or understand English and by their adherence to traditional Navaho practices that conflict with the children's new learning. In extreme cases, children consider traditional Navaho practices not only ignorant and superstitious, but evil.

Intercultural relations in the San Juan Valley, except in a few explosive situations in the past, have been generally quiet. Although in former days the Navahos harbored latent hostilities toward white people, these feelings remained submerged because of the infrequency of contacts. Earlier contacts with traders had been on the whole helpful in bridging the gap between Indians and white men.

Some traders who had had close relations with the Navahos in the past grew with the economic development of the area. They play an important part in the present contact situation and can further improve intercultural understanding by interpreting the Navaho adjustment problems to the increasing group of newcomers and by interpreting the new situation to the Navahos. This might be exemplified by what has already happened. The Fruitland trader who recruited Navaho labor in close association with the gas company is an excellent example. As chairman of the Board of County Commissioners and county Republican chairman, he knew the value of Indian votes and at the same time, although his views may have been biased by his party affiliation, taught many Navahos the value of the franchise. As the chairman of the local Board of Education, he was a proponent of education for Indian children and did much to get them into the public schools. Others have had similar status. In 1950 Farmington's mayor, city judge, and chief of police—men who had spent several decades as traders to the Navahos and thus were able to speak their language—were all active in their own ways in promoting intercultural understanding.

By 1954, as already indicated, there existed evidences of intergroup tension. On the one hand many whites, mostly persons who employed Navahos or worked with them, expressed considerable resentment over the Indians' irresponsible behavior. On the other hand, the Navahos began to feel that they were being discriminated against by employers and by the police. Many not so directly involved also began to stereotype Navaho behavior because of the activities of a few. The record of arrests appearing three or four times a week in the local newspaper revealed the same Navaho names. Although no open brawls occurred between Navahos and whites, the Indians were frequently arrested for fighting among themselves and for intoxication. The town's general growing pains were affecting the Navahos in particular. More generally, Oliver La Farge described the situation:

Farmington used to be one of the most delightful little towns or big villages in the United States. Everybody knew everyone. Nobody hurried.

Now Farmington has grown, all right. Minerals, oil, gas, have drawn the men and the money there. It is hustling, it is booming. Its drowsiness is ended, its streets are full of strangers, it is achieving what some believe to be the American dream.

Along with that have come the little items we have been reading about recently. . . . A whole series of ugly developments that would have been unthinkable 10 years ago.[31]

The repeal of the liquor law prohibiting sale of liquor to Indians, which many believed would tend to stop excessive drinking by Navahos, had so far worked in reverse. Navahos could now drink legally, but they continued to drink from bottles in back alleys and not at bars, probably because, as one said, "Drinks are cheaper by the bottle and I don't feel com-

[31] *Farmington Daily Times,* April 16, 1956.

fortable in bars." Furthermore, they continued to consume the entire contents of the bottle in town, because possession of alcoholic beverages on the reservation was still illegal. As a result Navahos exposed themselves to arrests for intoxication and reckless driving.

Here, as in all aspects of the adjustment situation, Navahos must be given opportunities to undo old habits and to learn to "define the situation" in the framework of the wider social context.

An examination of the present governmental approach to the problem indicates that serious consideration has been given to many of the factors which affected the outcome of the Collier program. The present approach, for example, is seen in the title of the present program, "The Long Range Program for Navajo-Hopi Rehabilitation." Specialists of all sorts in the technical fields have surveyed and resurveyed reservation resources. Even the tribe has hired consultants to check government findings. The program is many-faceted and supplied with what seem to be adequate funds. Public-works projects under way enable many families to live fairly comfortably, and off-reservation work satisfies the economic needs of others. Indeed, it is estimated that the total gross earnings from wages earned off and on the reservation by all Navahos during 1953 was $14,500,000; and in 1955 the Navahos received $35,000,000, of which only $4,000,000, or 11.4 per cent, was derived from reservation agriculture and stock raising.[32] The tabulation of available figures shows a total of approximately "23,000 placements made through the combined efforts of the Railroad Retirement Board, State Employment Services of Arizona and New Mexico, and the Branch of Placement and Relocation at Window Rock." [33]

[32] *The Navajo Yearbook*, Report no. VI, Fiscal Year 1957, pp. 92–93.
[33] *The Navajo Yearbook of Planning in Action*, Report no. V, 1955, p. 49.

Much progress has been made in the long-range program since the initial appropriation in 1951. The emphasis has been on the construction of school buildings, development of roads and trails, hospitals and health facilities, irrigation projects, soil and moisture conservation, range improvements, and resettlement on the Colorado River Irrigation Project. By 1954 approximately $34,000,000 had been appropriated.[34]

The Navahos are receiving immediate economic benefits in the form of wages. But the most important aspect of the program, the education of adult Navahos in their new way of life and in the value of the development of resources, is being neglected. Moreover, the continuing wagework opportunities, so badly needed during the 1930's and late 1940's, are today hampering the agricultural program. Yet the expansion of irrigation projects is regarded as most vital for the Navahos' long-range rehabilitation.

Because of the permanent nature of the water supply which has as its source the San Juan River, the major irrigation developments have occurred, and continue to expand, in the valley contiguous to the river. It is imperative that the water be used. Otherwise new developments may not materialize. As early as 1949 the tribal delegate from Fruitland recognized the political importance of using the river's water. At the Hearings before the Committee on Public Lands, House of Representatives, he said:

It is urgent that sufficient appropriations be made available so as to complete those units where it is necessary to protect valuable water rights, such as the San Juan River units. Failure to utilize these waters in the near future could very well result in the loss of valuable water rights.[35]

[34] *Ibid.,* p. 1.

[35] House of Representatives, Hearings before the Committee on Public Lands, Subcommittee on Indian Affairs, H.R. 3476, *To Promote the Rehabilitation of the Navajo and Hopi Tribes of Indians and for Other Purposes, April 18, 1949* (mimeographed at Window Rock, Ariz.).

It was not until 1951, however, that government and tribal leaders filtered the news down to the local farmers, who had neglected to cultivate their land because of their participation in wagework. Not only did wagework interfere with the agricultural activity of the established farms, but it interfered with the resettlement of Indians on newly created farms. By 1951 there were 400 additional acres ready for cultivation on the Fruitland Project. One assignment of 60 acres was turned over to an applicant, and the remainder was made available in smaller plots. But by 1955 only a few of those fields were being productively used.

Thus the three factors, a long-range program of rehabilitation, off-reservation work, and current irrigation projects, have to some extent been in conflict with each other.

The major part of the social life of the Fruitlanders continues to be carried out on the reservation, but the context of the larger situation must be considered. Their social life, already restructured by previous upsetting experiences, is now being geared to the pressures imposed upon it by the nationwide cash economy. Therefore, if the changing social structure is to be given a sound basis for its existence, it seems essential that new opportunities be stabilized. Ways must be discovered to orient the Navahos to their new way of life in order to render them less vulnerable to the rapid changes to which they are being exposed. The main task still belongs to the government, but, as John Collier so aptly said of government in 1947,

veritably hounded, by the exigent over-all requirements, it has not often dared to pause and to try to think through and feel through the problem of how the service and the issues can merge with each of the local communities, one by one. . . . The Indian Service has not had, or has not used, the means whereby it could reach the intellect and the psyche and the social opinion of the Navajos at the "grass roots." [36]

[36] John Collier, *Indians of the Americas* (New York: New American Library, 1947), p. 166.

The task is not as hopeless as it may sound, for the Navaho people themselves have become involved in their own rehabilitation. The view reflected by Tribal Chairman Paul Jones when he summarized a recent move by the Navaho Council to bring industry to the four-state reservation area is probably prophetic. "Wednesday we were studying grazing regulations. Those were symbolic of the traditional way of life. Thursday we discussed the new way of life." [37]

[37] *Farmington Daily News*, Dec. 9, 1955.

APPENDIX A

System of Subject Categories

I. Named Communities

  A. Shiprock
  B. Burnhams
  C. Farmington
  D. Other

II. Social Organization

  A. Religion and Supernatural

    1. Native
    2. Cults
    3. Protestants
    4. Catholics
    5. Other

  B. Education

    1. Government
    2. Off-reservation
    3. Mission
    4. Public school
    5. Other

  C. Government

    1. Fruitland-BIA
    2. Window Rock–BIA
    3. Washington
    4. Tribal
    5. Tribal-local
    6. State and County

  D. Leadership

  E. Kin Relationships

    1. Clan and extended family
    2. Nuclear family
    3. Husband-wife relationships
    4. Sibling relationships
    5. Marriage and separation

  F. Age and Sex Roles

    1. Infancy
    2. Childhood
    3. Adolescence and youth
    4. Adulthood
    5. Old age

  G. Social Stratification

H. Intergroup Relations
   1. Navaho-Government
   2. Navaho-other Indians
   3. Navaho-Spanish Americans
   4. Navaho-traders
   5. Navaho-Mormons
   6. Navaho-townspeople
   7. Navaho-others

I. Law and Social Control
   1. Formal
   2. Informal

J. Communication
   1. Formal
   2. Informal

K. Language

L. Rapport—Research Team and Community

III. Subsistence
   A. Technological Change
   B. Conservation
   C. Primary Industries
      1. Agriculture
      2. Crop production
      3. Animal husbandry
      4. Coal mining
      5. Other
   D. Secondary Industries
      1. Silversmithing
      2. Weaving
      3. Other
   E. Tertiary Industries
      1. Transportation
      2. Clerical, secretarial
      3. Service
      4. Other

F. Formal and Informal Labor Groups

G. Income and Disposition
   1. Wages and salaries
   2. Taxes
   3. Profits
   4. Disposition
   5. Consumption
   6. Savings
   7. Investments
      a. Productive
      b. Nonproductive

H. Exchange
   1. Prices
   2. Markets
   3. Monopolies
   4. Gift giving
   5. Medium of exchange
   6. Credit

I. Property and Contract
   1. Housing
   2. Nonresidential housing
   3. Other

J. Types of Work (nonfarm)
   1. Railroads
   2. Gas company
   3. Mines
   4. Government
   5. Corporation farms
   6. Construction
   7. Other

K. Food

L. Drink and Indulgence

M. Annual Cycle

N. Migration

IV. Survival and Fitness

  A. Daily Routine

  B. Health

    1. Morbidity
    2. Mortality
    3. Good health
    4. Medical facilities

  C. Recreation

  D. Nonmedical Practitioners

  E. Natural Environment

  F. Sex and Reproduction

  G. War and Peace

  H. Dress and Adornment

V. Personality

APPENDIX B

Proposed Working Agreement between the Window Rock Area Office and Cornell University

1. The primary role of the Cornell University Southwest Field Station Project at Fruitland, New Mexico, is to conduct research on human problems, cooperating with Tribal representatives, local Chapters and Indian Bureau officials in the application of scientific technical knowledge to programs which have to do with technological and social change. At Fruitland the Cornell group is especially interested in encouraging Navajos located in the Fruitland irrigation project to progress in agriculture, industry, self-government, and in transition into the broader society.

2. In order to facilitate the work of the Cornell Southwest Project, a working relationship between the Cornell group, the Navajo Tribe and the Window Rock Area Office is required. To meet this requirement, the Window Rock Area Office hereby and herewith agrees that:

(a) Representatives of the Cornell University Southwest Project shall be invited to attend meetings of the Shiprock Irrigation Project Coordinating Committee in an advisory capacity, and for purposes of having access to information.

(b) Representatives of the Cornell group shall be invited to serve in an advisory capacity or to function as members of sub-committees appointed or to be appointed by the Shiprock Irrigation Project Coordinating Committee.

(c) The Cornell group is hereby authorized to negotiate cooperative projects between themselves and Branches of the Area Office directly with the Branches concerned, and to carry out cooperative programs thus developed, with the approval of the Area Director.

(d) The Cornell group shall be given free access to non-classified documents in the official files at the Window Rock Area Office for purposes of information and research.

3. The Cornell Southwest Project agrees to:

(a) Submit annual progress reports in October covering the following subjects:

(1) The social effects of programmed and autonomous technical programs,

(2) Areas of friction and fit in the developments named in (1) above,

(3) Evaluation of programs and cooperative arrangements from the social science point of view,

(4) Recommendations for the following season's operation.

4. In order to facilitate the work of the Cornell Southwest Project to the greatest extent possible, the Navajo Tribe agrees to:

(a) Invite representatives of the Cornell Southwest Project to attend and participate in meetings of the Advisory Committee or other Tribal Council committees in the discussion of problems and programs which are concerned with or related to the work of the Cornell group.

(b) Give the Cornell group free access to non-classified information in the files of the Tribal Office for purposes of information or research by the Cornell group.

The above agreement shall become effective when it has been duly signed by the Area Director of the Window Rock Area Office, the Chairman of the Navajo Tribal Council, the duly authorized representative of the Cornell Southwest Project, and approved by the Commissioner of Indian Affairs.

APPENDIX C

Window Rock Area Office

The Indian Service personnel with closest relationships to the Fruitland Navahos were organized as follows in 1950:

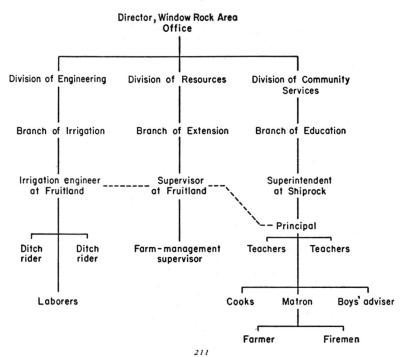

APPENDIX D

Staff of the Southwest Project, Cornell Studies in Culture and Applied Science

Alexander H. Leighton	Project director
John Adair	Field director, 1949–1952
Tom T. Sasaki	Field director, 1952–1956
Clifford Barnett	1950
Milton Barnett	1949
John Wood Collier, Jr.	1952–1953
Howard French	1953
Elizabeth Green	1949
Ralph Leubben	1952–1953
John Musgrave	1949
David L. Olmsted	1950
Seymour Parker	1954
William T. Ross	1952–1953
G. William Skinner	1948

Laila Shukry 1952
Philip Sottong 1952
Gordon F. Streib 1950–1951
Robert B. Textor 1950
Marc-Adelard Tremblay . 1952

Index